WHAT
GOD
HAS SAID
—— ABOUT
Humankind

LENN ZELLER

*A Bible study for personal reflection
or small group discussion.*

What God Has Said—About Humankind
by Lenn Zeller

Library of Congress Number: 2024932741
International Standard Book Number: 978-1-60126-907-2

Published by
Masthof Press
219 Mill Road | Morgantown, PA 19543-9516
www.Masthof.com

DEDICATION

Dedicated to the glory of God the Father,
Son and Holy Spirit

Table of Contents

INTRODUCTION

"When I consider Your heavens, the work of Your fingers, the moon and the stars, which You have set in place, what is man that You are mindful of him, the son of man that You care for him?" (Psalm 8:3-4)

Perhaps you have had the experience King David expressed in Psalm 8. This was a song of worship and praise, celebrating the great name of the Lord God Almighty:

"O Lord, our Lord,
how majestic is Your name in all the earth!"
(Psalm 8:1)

The image that comes immediately to mind upon reading this poem is of a person (David—or, perhaps us!) standing outside under a brilliant, clear night sky, gazing at the moon and stars above, and being awed by the size and grandeur of God's creation.

King David, who lived sometime around 1,000 B.C., could not possibly have known what science now tells us about that sky above. Astronomers say that our universe contains 2 trillion galaxies, each of which contains 100 billion stars, as well as numberless planets, moons, asteroids, comets, nebulae and other such objects.[1] The size alone is overwhelming, not to mention the beauty and magnificence of what God has made. Photos from telescopes sent into outer space transmitted back to earth show scenes of unimaginable complexity and beauty.

On a much simpler level, General Robert E. Lee once wrote as he rode through the Shenandoah mountains:

"I enjoyed the mountains as I rode along. The views are magnificent, the valleys so beautiful, the scenery so peaceful. What a glorious world Almighty God has given us."[2]

Such were the feelings of King David. I can identify with that myself. In fact, it was the magnificence of creation that first opened my heart to the One who created it all.

And in the face of all that glory, majesty and mystery, David asked a pertinent question … "What is man that You [God] are mindful of him? The son of man that You care for him?" (Psalm 8:4) Next to the immensity of this universe and all that it contains, who are we humans that God should even notice us, much less care about our existence, with its joys, sorrows, faults, failings, successes and victories?

That is the question that we will at least begin to address in this short work. What is man, and man's place in God's view? Who are we that we should be such a significant part of God's purposes and so dear to His heart? As such a miniscule speck in the whole of His creation, what is man that God should be mindful of us?

Before we go any further, a disclaimer is in order. The Bible's use of the word "man" is inclusive in many, if not most, places. It is a general, generic term that refers to humankind—men and women both. The Hebrew term in most instances is: ā·ḏām'.[3] It's the same as the name that was first given to Adam in Genesis 2:20. But in many instances, it is used to refer to humankind in general.

Some have argued that it is actually truer to the Bible to continue to use the word "man" as a term to refer to the entire human race, because that's what God Himself did in Genesis 5:

"This is the written account of Adam's line. When God created man, He made him in the likeness of God. He created them male and female and blessed them. And when they were created, He called them 'man'." (Genesis 5:1-2)

So, it is argued, perhaps correctly, that God Himself used the term "man" to refer to males and females both. In centuries past this would have been common practice and not worthy of discussion or explanation.

But in our modern culture, to refer to the whole of "humankind" as "man" or "mankind" is a matter of no small consternation for some. Therefore, in an attempt to be considerate of modern sensitivities, I will henceforth use the terms "humankind," "humanity," or "people" to avoid the charge of discrimination, prejudice or misogyny. Unless, of course, I am quoting Scripture directly (as above); then I will be faithful to the text as written.

That discussion aside, the question David raised will be the focus of this volume. What is humankind? Where did we come from and why are we here? What is our role in God's grand scheme of things? How are we different from all other creatures on earth? What does it mean to be human?

To consider such matters, we will look at Biblical passages in which God Himself speaks directly about humankind. What has God said about humankind is the title and the focus of this volume. Dr. Martyn Lloyd-Jones once said:

"To believe God means an utter, implicit confidence in what He has said about Himself and in what He has said about what He will do."[4]

We will assume an implicit confidence in what God has said, not only about Himself, but also about us. As in my books about what God has said about God, Jesus and the Holy Spirit, this too will not attempt to provide a full, systematic theology concerning humankind. Others have done that far better than I ever could.

Here we will simply study several passages in which God spoke specifically to the reality of humanity in His creation. It would make for an interesting study for an individual or for a small group. Hopefully, it will answer some questions we may have, but it may raise many more. That may spur you on to further study, which would be a good thing! Let's begin.

Part I

"Then God said, 'Let Us make man in Our image, in Our likeness, and let them rule over the fish of the sea and the birds of the air, over the livestock, over all the earth, and over all the creatures that move along the ground.' So God created man in His Own image, in the image of God He created him; male and female He created them." (Genesis 1:26-27)

In this first section we will consider several important issues that are raised in this one Biblical text. It's just two short verses, but there are some crucial phrases that are central to our discussion of humankind, so we will separate them out and address them one at a time.

CHAPTER 1

How Did We Get Here?

"Then God said, 'Let Us make man in Our image, in Our likeness, and let them rule over the fish of the sea and the birds of the air, over the livestock, over all the earth, and over all the creatures that move along the ground.' So God created man in His Own image, in the image of God He created him; male and female He created them." (Genesis 1:26-27)

"*I*n the beginning God created the heavens and the earth.*" (Genesis 1:1)* To any who are uncertain about how this vast universe with all its stars and solar systems came to be, the solution is given at the very beginning of the Bible. The answer is simple—God created it. Why is there something rather than nothing (the most basic question of philosophy)? The answer is simple—because God created it.

Genesis 1:1-27 describes how God spoke creation into being. "God said," and it was so. Where there once was nothing, by the eternal word of the Father now there was everything we see, feel, hear, taste and smell, plus so much more that we can't discern with our normal, natural senses.

It has become more and more clear that, based on scientific evidence, "the created order did not unfold in a mechanical way, but according to God's eternal decrees and attributes."[5] Secular scientists and theoreticians have tried heroically (and sometimes hysterically) to explain our existence in a way that does not require a Creator or Designer.

Dr. Carl Sagan, the late astronomer and avowed atheist, once proclaimed that:

"Since the birth of the universe could now be explained by the laws of physics alone, there was 'nothing for a creator to do,' and every thinking person was therefore forced to admit 'the absence of God'."

Like Dr. Sagan, secular scientists have desperately wanted to prove that there is no God and that humankind is the pinnacle of existence. It was Protagoras who proclaimed, *"Homo mensura"*—man is the measure of all things. But he was wrong. We are not. God is. More on that point later.

"Space plus time plus chance," is the secularistic explanation for the origin of the universe. It is both unscientific and unreasonable to think that the world somehow popped into existence by itself, being its own cause. The truth is that the more we learn and the deeper we go into the mechanics of even the simplest elements of life, the more complex we find them to be and the less likely it is that life somehow naturally formed from some primordial soup. In *Cosmic Blueprint*, physicist Paul Davies says …

"It is possible to perform rough calculations on the probability that the endless breakup and reforming of the [primordial] soup's complex molecules would lead to a small virus after billions of years."

He further says that it works out to be one chance in over ten to the two millionth power, a "mind-numbing number," which would be even harder to achieve than just happening to flip "heads on a coin six million times in a row."[6]

Even Abraham Lincoln, more than a century ago, was reported to have said:

"In view of the order and harmony of all nature we behold, it would have been more miraculous to have come about by chance than to have been created and arranged by some great thinking power."

More and more formerly materialist scientists are concluding that the possibility of the natural, random convergence of all the necessary processes involved in the creation of life in any form is improbable beyond imagination. Many are beginning to admit that there must have been a Divine Designer and Creator, just as the Bible has said all along.

> "The more we get to know of our universe, the more the hypothesis that there is a Creator God, who destined the universe for a purpose, gains in credibility as the best explanation of why we are here."[7]

The Biblical narrative of creation posits a time frame of seven days, which is a hotly debated topic even in Christian circles. Some sincere believers—such as John Calvin, William Henry Thornwell and Louis Berkhof—understand that description in a very literal sense of seven, twenty-four hour days as we now define them; the more strident of whom claim that if you do not take those words in their absolute literal sense, then you cannot possibly be a true Christian. Other equally sincere followers of Christ—Augustine, Aquinas, J. Gresham Machen, and Francis Schaeffer—argue that the original language is speaking of epochs or eras of undefined centuries, even millennia; the more strident of whom claim that if you do not take those words in that broader sense, then you cannot possibly be a true Christian.

> "That ought to give pause to those who employ a particular view of creation as a Litmus test for orthodoxy. Furthermore, the remarkable diversity of the major views of the six days ought to make us more cautious and humble in our judgments."[8]

We will not get into all the exegetical arguments on either side of that divide. That is beyond the scope of our study here. At the risk of offending both sides, may I say that I myself am not 100% sure either way. All I know is that God spoke creation into being and He did it in whatever time frame He so chose. Perhaps in eternity we will have the opportunity to have such things explained, displayed and clarified for us.

The point being, in either case, that it was God who spoke this creation into existence. It was not natural processes of biology, it was not evolution, creation did not just spring into existence by its own initiative. Isaac Newton, three centuries ago was enthralled by the beauty of our solar system. But he looked at the sun, planets and comets, and wrote that all this "could only proceed from the counsel and dominion of an intelligent and powerful Being."[9]

Could this be at least a small part of what Paul meant when he said:

> *"Now we see but a poor reflection as in a mirror; then we shall see face to face. Now I know in part; then I shall know fully, even as I am fully known." (1 Corinthians 13:12)*

As the Bible expresses it, creation was as follows:

Day 1 – creation of light, separation of the light from darkness
Day 2 – creation of the sky, seas and lands
Day 3 – creation of seed-bearing plants, vegetation, fruits
Day 4 – creation of the sun and stars of the sky
Day 5 – creation of birds and living creatures of the sea
Day 6 – creation of livestock, wild animals and creatures that
        move along the ground

But something else happened on that sixth day in addition to the creation of livestock and wild animals that is central to our discussion here. After all else was spoken into being, when all creation was primed and ready, God said,

> *"'Let Us make man in Our image, in Our likeness, and let them rule over the fish of the sea and the birds of the air, over the livestock, over all the earth, and over all the creatures that move along the ground.' So God created man in His Own image, in the image of God He created him; male and female He created them." (Genesis 1:26-27)*

So there you have it. The answer to the first question we might ask about our existence as humans—How did we get here?—is answered quite clearly. *God created us.* It was God who spoke *creation* into existence and it was God who spoke *humankind* into existence.

Our very existence began in the wisdom and counsel of the sovereign, infinite, almighty, triune God. *"Let Us make man."* Father, Son and Holy Spirit together planned and fashioned humanity. It was a mutual, cooperative plan within the Persons of God.

We are not here by accident. We are not the result of some random chemical process happening in some primordial ooze. Space aliens did not plant us here—yes, there really are those who propose such a thing! For example, Dr. Francis Crick, the extremely brilliant man who discovered DNA's double helix, was only too happy to offer the theory that it was perhaps aliens who brought life to earth. He even gave an imposing "scientific" name to this theory: "Directed Panspermia."[10]

It was not aliens! <u>God</u> created us! It was the triune God who put us here. As King David said it in Psalm 139:

"For You created my inmost being;
You knit me together in my mother's womb.
I praise You because I am fearfully and
wonderfully made;
Your works are wonderful, I know that full well."
(Psalm 139:13-14)

While David did not know the breadth and depth of the cellular and biological processes of conception and childbirth, which we now know, I am sure he knew the rudimentary elements of the "birds and the bees," as parents carefully explain them to their children. But the King did understand that above and beyond the biology of it stood God Himself, who makes it all happen and makes it function as it does. Without the hand of God, none of us would ever have been born. We are *all* fearfully and wonderfully made—by Almighty God.

As someone I heard say it recently, millions of sexual connections are made every day, but not all of them result in a pregnancy. We can describe the cellular processes, which result in human conception, but we cannot explain why those processes result in conception in some instances and not in others. Why do some conceive a child and others not? It's because of the will and purposes of God. God makes the conceptions happen.

Job repeated this truth in his own way:

> *"…what will I do when God confronts me? What will I answer when called to account? Did not He who made me in the womb make them? Did not the same One form us both within our mothers?" (Job 31:14-15)*

The prophet Isaiah spoke it as well:

> *"This is what God the* LORD *says—He Who created the heavens and stretched them out, Who spread out the earth and all that comes out of it, Who gives breath to its people, and life to those who walk on it …" (Isaiah 42:5)*

All of the above speak clearly to the fact that it is ultimately God who has caused us to be. He is the One who caused each and every one of us to be conceived and born.

And notice the divine counsel that took place within the Trinity before the creation of humankind. For all other aspects and facets of creation God simply spoke and it came to be. But for the creation of humankind, it appears that the Father, Son and Spirit consulted together to plan, conceive and complete our specific formation. There was a discussion between the three Persons of the Trinity. Some time was spent by Them in planning, coordinating and designing what these humans would be like once created.

It was a carefully thought-out plan of the Father, Son and Spirit as they worked together on this divine "project." As one commentator expressed it:

> "The uniqueness and superiority of man in the created order is underscored by the divine consultation which took place prior to his creation. *'Let Us make man in Our image and in Our likeness'* (1:28). Who is this that takes counsel together? Certainly

not angels. Man is never said to be created in the likeness of angels, and God is never said to take counsel with angels … the only satisfactory explanation of the plural can be that man is the product of the contemplation of the pluralistic godhead, i.e., the Father, Son and Holy Spirit."[11]

That tells us something about the intentionality and care with which we were created. Far from the chance result of random forces within a mindless expanse of an endless universe, as some believe, we were very carefully conceived and purposefully placed on earth by the deliberate plans of the Almighty. Nothing accidental about it!

The atheistic, materialistic view of humankind is, as author Randy Alcorn (who does not himself subscribe to this belief system, by the way) describes it:

"You are the descendant of a tiny cell of primordial protoplasm washed up on an empty beach three and a half billion years ago. You are the blind and arbitrary product of time, chance and natural forces. You are a grab-bag of atomic particles, a conglomeration of genetic substance. You exist on a tiny planet in a minute solar system in an empty corner of a meaningless universe."[12]

But that would mean our lives were totally random, meaningless and without purpose or reason. I know people, perhaps you do as well, who believe that our existence is random and meaningless, and that we must simply live the best lives we can until we die, and then it all ends. There is nothing to follow. How sad that would be!

As the late theologian and teacher Dr. R. C. Sproul said it:

"If indeed we came from the abyss of non-being and are being hurled relentlessly back to the abyss, what value, worth or dignity do we have? If our origin and destiny are meaningless, how can our lives now have any meaning?"

But we did *not* come from an "abyss of non-being." We came from the mind and hand of God Almighty! The meaning of our lives comes from the fact that God had a purpose in creating us, and He has a plan for our lives. We are important to Him. We are significant in His mind and heart. Even if we ourselves see nothing substantial or necessary in us, God does! Even if we view our own existence as trivial and meaningless, God does not.

Children even in loving families are sometimes told that they were an "accident." By that is meant that the parents were not planning to have anymore children than those they already had, or perhaps they were not anticipating having any children at all just yet. Nevertheless they somehow conceived and a child was born, beyond their plans or expectations. That child may have seemed an "accident" to the parents, but it was not a surprise to God. It was not a mishap or misfortune to Him, because He was the One who willed it to happen.

May I suggest that even a child born as a result of rape or incest—as immoral and horrible as those situations are—is not an accident to God. That child too is born by the plan, wisdom and grace of God and needs to be cherished as such. Whoever you are, whatever the circumstances and conditions of your physical birth, please know that you are here by God's sovereign choice, and no matter what anyone else may say, you are not an "accident" to Him.

We all long to be significant. We all want to count for something and be worthwhile. A character in the movie "Out of Africa" said, "There are some things that are worth something … I want to be one of them." We *all* want to be worth something.

It was the Lord God who formed you in your mother's womb. It was the Lord God who gave you breath and life. You are sacred and special to Him. He gave the life of His own Son, Jesus, on the cross to redeem you from your sins. He paid the ultimate price for you, out of love and grace.

Therein lies our dignity, true self-esteem and meaning. Therein lies our value and worth. We are not the result of random biological processes and we are no accident. Our origin and destiny are not meaningless. We are chosen and planned by our Creator God, and in Him we live and move and have our being. (Acts 17:28) That is what makes us who we are! This is how much God cares for and loves us:

"For God so loved the world that He gave His one and only Son, that whoever believes in Him shall not perish but have eternal life. For God did not send His Son into the world to condemn the world, but to save the world through Him." (John 3:16-17)

(?) QUESTIONS FOR CONTEMPLATION OR CONVERSATION

1. How has the secularistic explanation for the origin of the universe ("Space plus time plus chance") affected our culture and even our churches?

2. Do you think of your very existence in purely natural and biological terms, or as the result of a divinely inspired plan? Why? What difference does it make?

3. In what specific aspects of your life can you see that you were fearfully and wonderfully made?

4. On what do you base your significance? How has that worked for you—or not worked?

5. How would it affect the way we treat others to see them as people lovingly created by Almighty God? How would it change our attitude to think of them as such?

CHAPTER 2

In the Image of God

"Then God said, 'Let Us make man in Our image, in Our likeness, and let them rule over the fish of the sea and the birds of the air, over the livestock, over all the earth, and over all the creatures that move along the ground.' So God created man in His Own image, in the image of God He created him; male and female He created them." (Genesis 1:26-27)

The **second** thing to notice in our first Biblical text is that we were made in the image of God Himself.

"'Let Us make man in Our image, in Our likeness …'" (Genesis 1:26)

Genesis states that all other forms of life were created *"after their kind."*

"Let the land produce vegetation: seed-bearing plants and trees on the land that bear fruit with seed in it, <u>according to their various kinds</u>." (Genesis 1:11, emphasis mine)

"So God created the great creatures of the sea and every living and moving thing with which the water teems, according to their kinds, and every winged bird according <u>to its kind</u>." (Genesis 1:21, emphasis mine)

"God made the wild animals according to their kinds, the livestock according to their kinds, and all the creatures that move along the ground <u>according to their kinds</u>." (Genesis 1:25, emphasis mine)

In other words, the various types, species and categories of the animals, birds and fish were formed by God to be what they were and would be. No mixing and matching required, no species of one kind needing to develop into a species of a different sort, as the now-disproved theory of evolution used to say. An ape did not become a human. A fish did not crawl out of the sea and become a bird. God formed each animal to be what they were meant to be, according to their kind.

This in and of itself could be considered a Biblical detail that clearly contradicts the theory of evolution, which posits that each species was the result of millions of years of evolutionary processes. Here we are told that God created them, each after its own kind: terrestrial animals of all the various species and types—cattle capable of labor or domestication, wild animals, some with ravenous natures, and all the various forms of creeping things, from the huge reptiles to the seemingly insignificant caterpillars.[13]

But humanity was created *in the image and likeness of God*, a rather peculiar and profound distinction from all other forms of life. It is the source of what is sometimes called "human exceptionality." This is not a phrase of arrogant presumption, to put *ourselves* on a higher plane than other life forms. It is a term that speaks to the uniqueness of our specific creation as the human species, and of the place *God* has for us in His own purposes.

In fact, it is even mentioned twice for emphasis, using two different words. The first word for "image" is the Hebrew *tselem*, which means "form" or "likeness."[14] The second word translated as "image" in the NIV ("*likeness*" in some translations) is the Hebrew *demût*. It can be translated as "similitude," "figures resembling," or even "likeness." So we can clearly see that their meanings are very similar.

In both cases, the idea in general is of a rough copy or an image, such as a graphic representation of a building before its construction or a sculpted representation of an animal.[15] Often in the newspapers you will see an artist's rendering of a building that is to be constructed. It's not the building itself, of course, but it basically shows what the structure may look like upon completion. That's the sense of these words.

Even a painted portrait is an image or likeness of a person, accurate only to the limits of the talent of the artist painting it. If I were to commission an artist to paint a portrait of my wife, I would most likely not contact an impressionist artist, such as Monet and Renoir. As famous and talented as they may have been, if their rendering of my wife would be similar to other works of theirs that I have seen, it would not be a very accurate or detailed image of my beloved. I would more likely seek out an artist who is able to produce capable and realistic portraits. But even the best are mere renderings or representations, and not the person themselves.

The real significance here is in the use of the double reference. That kind of repetition is a common Biblical method of emphasizing a point. So this is evidently important and worth our notice. Humans, unlike all other living creatures on earth about whom this was *not* said, were made in the likeness and image of God.

So <u>how</u>, you might ask, are we in the image of God? It's not in our appearance. God is spirit, as Jesus told us in John:

> *"God is spirit, and His worshipers must worship in spirit and in truth." (John 4:24)*

God does not have a physical body like ours, even though He is often depicted by the Biblical writers in anthropomorphic terms. That is done merely to express things about God in words that we can understand. It nowhere describes His actual being or appearance. He is not a kindly-looking old man in a white robe and with a long beard. That is an artist's rendering, based on their own imagination. In fact, God Himself said, "... *you cannot see My face, for no one may see Me and live.*" (Exodus 33:19-20) So it can be easily surmised that we are not created in God's image *physically*. Something else must be in mind here when it said we are made in God's image.

Scholars and theologians have described this in a wide variety of terms. The ancient church fathers and the Reformers saw this as an essentially spiritual reality. The commentary of Jamieson, Fausset, and Brown speaks in terms of the "moral dispositions of our soul," which at the time of our creation (Adam and Eve) was pure and righteous.[16] That, of course, became marred by sin, but it will one day be restored.

> *"You were taught, with regard to your former way of life, to put off your old self, which is being corrupted by its deceitful desires;*

to be made new in the attitude of your minds; and to put on the new self, created to be like God in true righteousness and holiness." (Ephesians 4:22-24).

Others speak of humankind's "intellectual, spiritual, volitional, and ethical capacity."[17] God implanted in our hearts, minds and souls depths of understanding, perception and capacity for relationship with ourselves, with others and with God that other creatures simply were not given.

"This means that as image-bearers we can hear and receive God's Word. No other creature can do that. This also means that we are responsible, moral, spiritual beings."[18]

In short the combination "image and likeness" refers to all that sets man apart from the animal kingdom.

God did not say of the birds of the air, "Let Us make them in Our image." God did not say of the cattle of the field, "Let Us make them in Our image." No whale or dolphin, no dog or cat, no eagle or owl was made in the image of God.

Contrary to the worldview of radical "animal rights" activists, no animals have the ability to make moral choices between good and bad, right and wrong. Animals do not have the intellectual capacities of humans to understand life and history or to analyze the situations in which they find themselves to any appreciable degree. Animals are not made in the image of God like we are. Does that give us the right to treat animals with callous abuse or disregard? No, of course not. But neither does it put those creatures on the moral and ethical level of humans.

Activists have in recent years filed lawsuits in court on behalf of certain animals (in one case an elephant!) claiming for them the same legal status as human beings. They seek to put animals on the same moral and legal level as humans—or perhaps drag humans down to the level of animals.

Animal Rights for some is an ideology that claims humans and animals are morally equal because both can suffer. Hence, that which is done to animals should be judged as if the same actions were done to people.[19] PETA

(People for the Ethical Treatment of Animals) have compared the eating of meat to the sufferings of the Jews in the Holocaust.

I care deeply about the treatment of animals and hate to see any animal abused. Nevertheless, I also believe in "human exceptionalism" and would disagree with those who put animals on par with humans. In God's grand scheme of the universe, humans are made in God's image, and animals, birds and fish are not.

> *"What is man that You are mindful of him,*
> *the son of man that you care for him?*
> *You made him a little lower than the heavenly beings*
> *and crowned him with glory and honor."*
> (Psalm 8:4-5)

It was God who created humankind a little lower than heavenly beings and crowned us with glory and honor. The Bible does not say such things about birds, animals or fish. Any view we hold of our own self-worth and self-esteem should take into account the valued place we hold in God's creation. Secularists and atheists would say that humankind has no innate or distinctive value. We are merely the result of random forces and biological processes and therefore have no intrinsic or eternal significance. God says something very, very different about us, and that is what gives us reason for self-esteem. It's in and because of God, not us.

According to the timeless Word of God in the Bible, we can safely say that humankind is set apart from and above all other creatures of God's creation. That tells us something of our exalted and honored place in creation, and the uniqueness of our very being. We are not on level with animals, nor they with us. This is something else that should inform our view of who we are in God's sight.

Now, of course, it is true that the fall into sin, by the disobedience of Adam and Eve in the Garden of Eden (Genesis chapter 3), and the sin of every human being since then, has significantly marred the divine image in all of us, as it is described above. We are now not who we were created to be. But the seed of that divine image still resides in each of us.

And for those who have turned to God through repentance of their sins and by trusting in Jesus Christ as their Savior, that image of God is slowly but surely being restored. Like an artist who painstakingly restores a painting that has been damaged, and returns it to its created glory, so God is patiently working on those who are His to restore in us His own image and likeness.

The Apostle Peter, in his second New Testament epistle challenged us to *"grow in the grace and knowledge of our Lord and Savior Jesus Christ. To Him be glory both now and forever! Amen." (2 Peter 3:18)*

And Paul, in his second letter to the Corinthians said:

> *"And we, who with unveiled faces all reflect the Lord's glory, are being transformed into His likeness with ever-increasing glory, which comes from the Lord, who is the Spirit." (2 Corinthians 3:18)*

Both these and other New Testament passages tell us that we as believers are growing daily in the image of Christ and that God is working to transform us into His likeness in ever increasing measure.

One glorious day that process will be completed and the image of God that has been so tarnished by our sin will be restored to its fullness. What a great day that will be!

> *"...being confident of this, that He who began a good work in you will carry it on to completion until the day of Christ Jesus." (Philippians 1:6)*

Until then, it is our responsibility to cooperate with the Spirit and the Word of God in a gradual process theologians call "sanctification," and to grow in the grace, wisdom and glory of God.

Are you faithfully reading the Scriptures, first and foremost, but also some of the plethora of good, solid Christian books and materials that are out there? Are you humbly allowing God to challenge and change you? Are you worshipping regularly and sitting under the teaching of a faithful, Biblical pastor? Are you finding ways to serve God in your church and community? All these, and more, are ways that we can *"continue to work out [our] salvation with fear and trembling ... " (Philippians 2:12)*

Base your self-image on who and what *God* says you are, on how unique in all of creation you are as a human being, on your place in His plans and purposes, and in your ultimate place in His kingdom by your faith and submission to Him. You are not a meaningless speck of dust in an infinite universe. You are a child of the living God, uniquely created and loved by the Creator. Turn to Him, through faith in His Son, Jesus, and live the life you were meant to live!

? QUESTIONS FOR CONTEMPLATION OR CONVERSATION

1. What does it mean to you to be created in the image of God? In what ways can His image be seen in who you are and how you live your life?

2. How do you understand the term "human exceptionality"? Is that a positive or a negative concept for you? Why?

3. In what ways do some people take their concern for the animal kingdom too far? Not far enough?

4. Does humankind have any innate or distinctive value? Why?

5. What are you doing to grow in the image of God and to grow in wisdom and grace? What more could you do?

CHAPTER 3

Let Them Rule

"Then God said, 'Let Us make man in Our image, in Our likeness, and let them rule over the fish of the sea and the birds of the air, over the livestock, over all the earth, and over all the creatures that move along the ground.' So God created man in His Own image, in the image of God He created him; male and female He created them." (Genesis 1:26-27)

Thirdly, please note the phrasing in our text above which speaks to humankind's dominion over the earth:

"… let them rule over the fish of the sea and the birds of the air, over the livestock, over all the earth, and over all the creatures that move along the ground."

The word for "rule" is the Hebrew word *rā·dā(h)*. It means "to rule over, dominate, direct, lead, control, subdue." In other words, "to manage or govern an entity, people or government with considerable or forceful authority."[20]

It's a word that is used often in the Bible to refer to a people conquered and subdued by an invader. It's used to describe people who are subjected to slavery. In other words, it speaks of total and absolute control of one over another.

"Then David ordered all the leaders of Israel to help his son Solomon. He said to them, 'Is not the Lord your God with you? And has He not granted you rest on every side? For He has handed the inhabitants of the land over to me, and the land is subject to the Lord and to His people." (1 Chronicles 22:17-18, emphasis mine)

David was a military genius, and his conquests were numerous and vast. He realized, of course, that it was God who gave him the ability, opportunity and strength to accomplish such victories.

> *"It is God who arms me with strength*
> *and makes my way perfect.*
> *He makes my feet like the feet of a deer;*
> *He enables me to stand on the heights.*
> *He trains my hands for battle;*
> *my arms can bend a bow of bronze.*
> *You give me Your shield of victory,*
> *and Your right hand sustains me;*
> *You stoop down to make me great.*
> *You broaden the path beneath me,*
> *so that my ankles do not turn."*
> *(Psalm 18:32-36)*

As David said, it was the LORD who handed the peoples of the nations over to the Israelites, and it was to God that those nations were ultimately subjected. But those nations were given by God to be ruled and controlled by Israel in His name and as agents of His dominion.

In much the same way, we are called by the LORD to "rule over" the other created beings (Genesis 1:26) and "subdue" the earth (Genesis 1:28). Humans have been given the authority and command of God to represent Him in the care of His creation. We are, in a sense, caretakers of the Lord's property, or to use the Christian jargon, "stewards."

Certainly we must do so in a careful, responsible and sensible way, following the guidance and command of God. We are not to run roughshod over the earth and pollute or destroy it without thought, or to treat the creatures of the earth with disdain, violence and contempt. Dominion does not mean abuse, misuse or maltreatment.

I hate reading stories of people who abuse animals. Photos in the news of animals that have been starved or abused by their owners break my heart. I think those who do such things deserve to be prosecuted to the full extent of the law.

Furthermore, numerous species of animals, mammals, birds and fish—think whales, bison, bald eagles and many more—have been taken to the edge of extinction by human over-hunting and greed. Many others have long since totally disappeared from this earth. That is not what I would call faithful or careful dominion.

Still further, I hate seeing the amount of trash lying along the roadsides we drive, from people who carelessly toss their waste out the window as they speed along. We live in a beautiful, mountainous area, with lovely scenery around every turn. It saddens us to think that people have such little concern for such natural beauty that they would litter so inconsiderately. Some even throw full garbage bags of trash by the roadside!

We recently passed a sign along a road that said "Littering: $300 fine." The side of the road was practically covered by cups, bottles, bags and other debris that people had thrown from their cars and trucks. I thought that $300 for each instance would amount to a tidy sum for the township in question. That is not faithful or careful dominion.

It saddens me to see pollution pouring out of industrial smokestacks, or out of the exhaust pipes of cars and trucks. I don't like seeing houses, buildings, properties or lands decimated and left to decay. When God told us to subdue and rule over the earth, that's not what He was talking about, I am quite sure.

He meant, I believe, to freely use it for our benefit, but also to take great care in how we do that. It belongs to Him, after all. We are just caretakers under His authority. Knowing and believing in the divine origins and ownership of all creation, Christians should be more concerned than anyone else about the environment and the conservation of the earth; without carrying that to the extremes to which some people are prone.

In times past, for a variety of reasons, people have graciously allowed us the use of one of their vehicles for a certain period of time while ours was in the garage. We were permitted and encouraged to use it as needed and to treat it as our own. But we never thought of that borrowed vehicle as our property. It belonged to our friend. We just had use of it for a time. And so we treated it with great care. I was always afraid that we would have an accident and damage or dent it, and would have to return it to the owner marred and lessened in value. Thankfully that never happened.

Such is the reality of Christian stewardship. We are not the owners of this earth or anything on or in it. We have been given the charge to manage and care for what belongs to God Himself. He is the Owner, and our challenge is to enjoy it so that we make full use of the resources without causing undue damage or harm to creation, remembering that it all belongs to Him. As God's Word says:

> *"The earth is the LORD's, and everything in it,*
> *the world, and all who live in it;*
> *for He founded it upon the seas*
> *and established it upon the waters." (Psalm 24:1-2)*

> *"I have no need of a bull from your stall*
> *or of goats from your pens,*
> *for every animal of the forest is Mine,*
> *and the cattle on a thousand hills.*
> *I know every bird in the mountains,*
> *and the creatures of the field are Mine.*
> *If I were hungry I would not tell you,*
> *for the world is Mine, and all that is in it."*
> *(Psalm 50:9-12)*

Biblically, we are allowed and even commanded to make use of the resources, lands, assets and benefits God has placed in our hands, and in some sense the advancements humankind has made over the centuries are remarkable. Humankind has made great progress in animal husbandry, farming, mining, architecture, medicine and more. Many of those discoveries were made by Christians seeking to serve God by properly managing His creation. Our use of the many and varied elements and God-given endowments of His creation has resulted in longer, healthier, safer lives on many fronts.

As one commentator says it:

> "Man has been given dominion over both herbage (Genesis 2:15) and animals (Genesis 2:20). Human beings have the God-given authority to chop down trees, build buildings, do-

mesticate animals, and eat meat. Human beings also have the responsibility to do those things responsibly."[21]

On the other end of the environmental spectrum, there are those who believe the only way for the earth to be properly cared for is to remove the presence of human beings altogether. That would return the earth to a "natural" state and remove the negative influence of humanity's abuses. There are some who literally propound such an idea.

Admittedly, keeping a good balance between abuse and proper stewardship of the earth without falling to either extreme can sometimes be difficult. I read recently in *World Magazine* a thoughtful story about deep sea mining in the Pacific Ocean. It seems that scientists have found an "exotic community" of newly discovered sea creatures including anemones as long as a man's arm and 3-foot-long "gummy squirrel" sea cucumbers, which sport a sail-like tail and come in a myriad of colors. They are amazing and beautiful creatures most of us will never see and would never imagine.

At the same time, these innumerable sea creatures happen to live in an area filled with polymetallic nodules containing "manganese, cobalt, nickel, copper, zinc and rare earth minerals, all vital for making the rechargeable batteries that undergird the global push toward green energy."[22] Such minerals are extremely valuable and desperately sought after.

We need those kinds of minerals if we want to lessen our dependence on fossil fuels, as some insist we must do to "save the planet." Yet to get at those necessary minerals we would have to disturb the habitat of those astonishing sea organisms. How do we balance pressing economic requirements with real environmental concerns? The answers to a situation like this are not easy to find.

Another example might be the coal industry. Our home is in the center of Pennsylvania "coal country." In the search for this vital element, mountains have been defaced, tunnels dug under the ground, water tables impacted, and one notable underground mine very near to our home was accidently ignited and has burned for decades, spewing dangerous fumes into the atmosphere. One whole town situated over it had to be torn down and the people moved away for their own health and safety.

At the same time, that coal is a vital source of heating, industrial energy and electricity, and without it multitudes of people and industries will suffer, and suffer greatly. That coal is absolutely necessary on a variety of levels, and there is enough of it just in Pennsylvania to last this nation a hundred years. But the economy of this region has fallen precipitously as our government has tried to completely shut down the coal industry over its concern for "global warming." So where is the balance?

Certainly mistakes have been made across the ages, abuses have occurred, animals have been hunted to extinction, lands have been deeply and perhaps permanently marred. This cannot be denied. At the same time, real human need is sometimes in the scales and the resources in question are unquestionably essential to the well-being of humankind. A reasonable balance is sometimes difficult to find. How do we exercise responsible dominion over God's creation, protecting wildlife and ecological balances while at the same time making use of God-given resources for the betterment of humankind? The answers are not always easy to find.

As Christians, we should be at the forefront of seeking solutions to such quandaries. Of all people, we should be seeking to honor God by being faithful stewards of His creation. Our dominion and rule should be careful, sensitive, caring and positive, using the resources God has placed in our hands to benefit humankind and yet protect, as much as possible, the creation itself.

QUESTIONS FOR CONTEMPLATION OR CONVERSATION

1. What does the command to rule over creation mean to you? How is it expressed in your daily life?

2. Do you think of yourself as a caretaker of God's earth? How does this affect your behavior and use of His resources?

3. Why should Christians be more concerned than anyone else about the environment and the conservation of the earth?

4. How can we find a good balance between abuse and proper stewardship of the earth without falling to extreme? How can we choose between conservation and properly using God's resources?

5. What specific things do you do to ensure that your dominion and rule are careful, sensitive and positive?

CHAPTER 4

Male and Female

"Then God said, 'Let Us make man in Our image, in Our likeness, and let them rule over the fish of the sea and the birds of the air, over the livestock, over all the earth, and over all the creatures that move along the ground.' So God created man in His Own image, in the image of God He created him; male and female He created them." (Genesis 1:26-27)

Fourthly, in this same Biblical paragraph, we might make note of the fact that God created us as male and female.

"So God created man in His Own image, in the image of God He created him; male and female He created them." (Genesis 1:26-27)

This clearly states that humans are created in two types, sexes or genders: male and female. Two genders, not untold multiples, as some now argue. We'll get to that in a moment. Sexuality and gender were created by God as a gift. Male and female were designed to be different in many ways, the same in others, and to complement one another emotionally, spiritually, physically and sexually.

Men and women are equal but complementary. We need each other. We are not like the two halves of an hourglass, which may be exchanged for each other without anyone noticing the difference.[23]

And we do work very well together when we live under the lordship of God the Father and according to His parameters for us. It is a marvelous thing when we follow the instructions He has given us in His Word to the best of our ability. The late Dr. Larry Crabb spoke of the design of God in creation and the power and joy of His people who live by this design.[24] When it is done as divinely designed, the relationship between male and female is a wonderful thing to behold! The route to joy is not to deny, mini-mize or reject who we are as a male or a female, but to embrace our created design and celebrate the differences.

Males have certain physical, emotional and intellectual gifts; females do, too. But they are not always the same. In fact, Larry Burkett used to say that in a marriage, if the two parties are exactly the same in every way, one of them is unnecessary. As many studies have shown, men "tend to value independence and mastery as the route to feeling complete and able to move confidently through life. Women, on the other hand, seem more concerned with developing close relationships ... The man talks of feeling complete, the woman of feeling attached."[25] Those differences need to be understood and enjoyed, not denied.

As there is unity within the three Persons of the Trinity—Father, Son and Spirit—being made in God's image (previously discussed) means that we, too, were made to live in relationship and unity with God and with oth-ers. The primary and most full way in which this happens in the earthly sense is within the bond of marriage, between one man and one woman. It is here that we most closely approach the perfect oneness of the Holy Trinity.

This is not to say that someone who is single, widowed or otherwise alone, is not a viable or significant human being, or that they cannot experi-ence deep relationship. But within the lifelong commitment of marriage we most closely reflect the oneness of the trinity.

Please note that marriage, as God created and instituted it, is between one man and one woman:

> "But for Adam no suitable helper was found. So the LORD God caused the man to fall into a deep sleep; and while he was sleeping, He took one of the man's ribs and closed up the place with flesh. Then the LORD God made a woman from the rib He had taken out of the man, and He brought her to the man.

> "The man said, 'This is now bone of my bones and flesh of my flesh; she shall be called 'woman,' for she was taken out of man.' For this reason a man will leave his father and mother and be united to his wife, and they will become one flesh." (Genesis 2:20-24)

Adam's joy and relief is palpable in his comments above. This woman was at last the one who was suitable for him and who could live with him in intimacy, unity and faithfulness. After viewing and naming all the other creatures on earth, Adam was still essentially and emotionally alone. He was thrilled with the gift of the woman to be his companion and co-worker (helper) in God's garden.

In a skit we once performed for our church's Vacation Bible School, when Adam first saw Eve, he was so happy that he shouted, "Whoa, man!" Then he said, "That's it, I'll call her 'Whoa-man,' or maybe just 'woman'."

This is just what God planned when He ordained the institution of marriage in the first place: one man and one woman living in a joyous, intimate, lifelong commitment to each other, to love and cherish, to have and to hold, till death do they part, each contributing their unique strengths and personal qualities to create an amazing whole, in the service of God's purposes for humanity.

God knew that we would need that kind of partnership to survive in this fallen, disjointed world, even in addition to His own presence and care. It's true that we need *Him*, most of all; but we need each other, too, in order to flourish as He has designed temporal life for us and to faithfully complete the work He has given us.

Notice that as God created and ordained it, marriage was not between two men, or between two women, or any other combination of multiples as is now being urged. Our society has redefined marriage as pretty much any combination of people and sexes one desires. In God's plan, it was (and still is) one man and one woman. Period. As Christopher Ash said it in his book, *Married for God*:

> "Marriage is between one man and one woman. This means that it is heterosexual rather than homosexual, and that it is monogamous rather than polygamous. It is heterosexual because this is how God has made us."

This special relationship is the clearest image of the Godhead we can experience on this earth. Within that relationship, we all have specific roles to play. "God created man and woman equal in value and personhood, and equal in bearing His image, but both creation and redemption indicate some distinct roles for men and women in marriage and in the church."[26] As we each do our God-given part, we strengthen the whole and enjoy the full benefits of the relationship between male and female.

It is this idea of distinct roles that drives feminists and progressives wild, and has been turned into a point of contention by those who are determined to reject and disobey God at every turn. Spiritual headship for the husband is anathema to many, who see it as an excuse for severe authoritarianism and even abuse.

To be sure, there are some cases where this does indeed happen, and that is very sad. But those abuses do not deny that this is the way God ordained it and when lived properly with mutual love and respect, it is the best of this world's reflections of God Himself.

Our contemporary culture is attempting to redefine marriage itself, and even who and what we are as men and women in abject defiance of God Almighty, sovereign Creator and ruler of all things and all people. Let there be no mistake—the effort to redefine or even destroy the institutions of marriage and the family is an attempt to rebel against the sovereignty of the LORD God Almighty. So are the current attempts to redefine the concepts of gender and sexuality.

During a recent hearing before a United States Senate committee, someone who had been appointed to a high government position was being interviewed in a Senate confirmation hearing, to be tested for their fitness for the job at hand. One of the Senators asked her a simple question: "What is a woman?" The candidate hesitated greatly, so the Senator kindly repeated the question. Finally, the nominee stammered that she couldn't answer that question. The Senator was incredulous. (As was I when I heard this reported later on the television news!) "You can't tell me what a woman is?" he exclaimed. The nominee replied that she could not (even though she is one), not in this context, and offered the excuse that she was not a biologist.

Now, I can't say why this appointee was unable (or unwilling, for whatever reasons) to answer this simple question, though I have my suspicions. And I don't know what context she was referring to that would have precluded answering such a direct query. But it does illustrate that in our modern western culture there is great confusion about such matters.

For the benefit of that particular nominee, who was subsequently approved by the way, a woman is a female human being. In biological terms, a woman is a human with two x chromosomes in each female cell; whereas a man is a human with one x chromosome and one y chromosome in each male cell. It's not all that complicated.

Genetically and biologically the female gender is quite easy to identify and define, as is the male. And that's not even mentioning the obvious physical characteristics of each that most often distinguish males from females. Notwithstanding the countless stated sexual preferences of human beings these days, and in spite of the numerous ways people may choose to identify themselves, there are really only two genders. And "the science" bears this out.

But there has arisen in our contemporary world a great debate about such issues as male and female. There are those who now claim that gender is a fluid matter of one's own choosing. No matter what our biological, cellular reality happens to be, there are some who say we can "identify" as any gender (or type of being, for that matter) we may so choose. I heard some women being interviewed on television blithely claiming that one was in reality a robin and the other a cardinal. They identified themselves as birds, not humans! The interviewer did not ask about their diet, however. I doubt those girls ate worms for breakfast!

Some (such as Google Search) list as many as 72 or even 87 gender identities: agender, bigender, gender expansive, gender fluid, gender outlaw, omnigender, polygender, pangender, transgender, trans man and trans male (what's the difference?), trans female and trans woman (again, what's the difference), blurgender, collgender, deliciagender and many, many more. I don't even know what many of those terms mean, and I doubt anyone else does either. By the way, my computer's spellcheck doesn't know those words, either—almost all of them are highlighted as misspelled words! Perhaps that's because they are not legitimate words at all!

One author reported:

"One person explained, 'I'm not a girl or a boy, I'm a gender smoothie, I mix it all up together.' Another stated that he preferred not to be identified as male or female. Instead, he preferred to be called a tractor. And we are supposed to embrace this [nonsense] as normal?"[27]

Others try to distinguish between the sex of a person and their gender identity. Sex refers to the biological characteristics of the person's sex organs, hormones and chromosomes, but they say that gender is non-binary and is rather a wide spectrum. Others argue—rather vehemently—that what you choose to think you are, that is what you literally are. I suppose I would have to admit that you have the right to think of yourself in whatever terms you may so choose. However, that does not change the reality of your God-given humanity.

It was reported that Abraham Lincoln, in a debate with a political opponent, asked the opposing politician how many legs a cow has. The man said, "Four, obviously." Lincoln said, "If you count her tail as a leg, then how many legs does she have?" His opponent replied, "Well, then I guess she has five legs." Lincoln said, "No, she still only has four legs. You can call her tail anything you want, but it doesn't change the fact that she has four legs."

That speaks directly to our "woke" world of today. You can call a man a woman, or a tractor, but he is still a man. You can call a woman a man, or a bird, or an animal. She is still a woman. Men cannot get pregnant and bear a child, as some claim.

Satirist Seth Dillon, of Babylon Bee, said it this way:

> "We are told by people with straight faces … that men can become women and women can become men and that sex is 'assigned at birth' (as though doctors observing a naked newborn are just making their best guess). We're told men can become pregnant and 'chest feed'."

He also quotes healthline.com, which answers the question, "Can men get pregnant?" by saying:

> "Yes, it's possible for men to become pregnant and give birth to children of their own. In fact, it's probably a lot more common than you might think."[28]

Are we supposed to take such nonsense as reality? This is the insanity of our culture today, calling a tail a leg and thinking that it is therefore so. Our culture thinks that you can believe yourself to be whatever you choose, in spite of biological, physical reality. This has led to many puzzling, confounding, alarming and even perilous situations that threaten the very fabric of our society. The ramifications are enormous, should we continue down that slippery slope.

Just one example is the trend to allow males who identify as females to use the women's bathrooms and locker rooms, and even to compete in women's sports. Biological males are now winning championships and setting records in women's sports. I've never heard of that happening in the opposite case! Some women have tried to compete on male teams or, for example, against males in a PGA golf tournament. They rarely—if ever—are able to even be competitive. The male physique has too much of an advantage.

In my humble estimation, this is the height of madness. Women's sports are for women. It gives them a chance to compete on equal footing with other women. To open women's sports to males is to deny women their rightful place and to belittle their efforts and achievements.

And to allow a male into the spaces once rightfully and respectfully reserved for women is courting abuse and sexual assault. There will always be those who will take advantage of a situation like that to gratify their own wicked desires and fantasies. Cases have already been reported of men entering women's bathrooms or locker rooms, claiming to be "transgender," and then committing sexual assault. So were they really transgender as they claimed, or were they taking advantage of the madness of our culture to satisfy their own violent perversions?

A better path, I would suggest, would be to turn to God for our answers and definitions. What is a human being in the mind's eye of the one Who created us? What is a man and what is a woman to God Almighty? The Bible is clear about these things. God created us male and female. There are two sexes and two genders. Period.

In my humble opinion, the transgender movement is all about defiance of God, at least for most of those who seriously claim it as their own. This is not to deny that in some cases gender dysphoria is a very real thing, and confusion about one's sexuality is a real issue. Nor is it to minimize or mock those who have sincere issues and questions along these lines. Nor is it to disregard the powerful effects of peer pressure and social constraints that push impressionable young people in these culturally celebrated directions.

But my suspicion is that for many who are embracing this temporary fad and bowing to pressure from their peers and their society, transgenderism is a willful, defiant rejection of the sovereign authority of Almighty God. It is fallen people shaking a closed fist toward heaven and saying to God, "You will not tell me who or what I am! I will be whatever *I* choose for myself. You will have no authority over me!"

And so, submitting to the madness of the culture, even many so-called scientists and many once respected doctors and hospitals are offering what they call "compassionate gender-affirming care," using puberty blockers, cross-sex hormones and radical, body-altering surgeries to under-age children expressing gender confusion.

One pediatrician admitted that "boys who believe in Santa Claus can also believe the fantasy that they can become girls if enough cross-sex hormones are pumped into their prepubescent bodies."[29] Others become defensive and angry at those who simply raise legitimate questions about this whole issue. At the time of this writing, hospitals, therapists and surgeons are making a lot of money offering questionable treatments and surgeries.

Gender transition is the latest fad that many are promoting, even some therapists, physicians and school personnel, often being careful to hide it from the child's parent, who will most likely object. But after all the treatments and surgeries are over, when the child is older and realizes that they are indeed what God created them to be (as many if not most eventually do), they regret what they have done to their bodies. Unfortunately it is literally impossible to undo the damage. They find that to "de-transition" is not at all what they were told. They will never be the same.

But as one commentator opined, once the insurance companies have had enough of this folly and decide not to fund this dubious "medicine" any longer, it will quickly fade into oblivion, as have other "health" fads of the past, because there will be no more money to be made on it. This has begun to happen already in several European nations. Unfortunately this passing mania will leave a trail of broken lives in its wake.

It will not end well for us if we continue to insist on this untenable way of thinking and this irrational behavior, even from medical professionals who should (and perhaps do) know better. We need to allow God to define His own creation. We need to turn to His Holy Word for our definitions. That is where we will find the answers.

Compassionate care and realistic counsel is what a confused person needs, not hormone blockers and radical, irreversible surgery. Offering a confused child or teen a kind, listening ear, wise and caring Biblical counsel, and pointing them to Jesus who wants to save them and heal them in their heart and soul is what is called for. Helping a child or young adult to embrace and celebrate who they were created to be is much more helpful. That and a call to humble obedience to the Word of the Creator, and His will for our individual lives. We are happier and healthier when we live in accord with the way God created us, not when we reject and deny His plan and order.

"So God created man in His Own image, in the image of God He created him; male and female He created them." (Genesis 1:26-27)

Special Note: This seems an appropriate place to add an important note: All that we have been saying thus far speaks to the *sacredness* of human life. The fact that we were created by God; made in His image; given a significant role in tending His garden; and carefully differentiated into male and female, shows that to God, humankind is a very special, even hallowed part of His creation.

In Genesis 9, God based His law against murder on the fact that humankind was made in His image:

"And for your lifeblood I will surely demand an accounting. I will demand an accounting from every animal. And from each man, too, I will demand an accounting for the life of his fellow man. Whoever sheds the blood of man, by man shall his blood be shed; for in the image of God has God made man." (Genesis 9:5-6)

I would even argue, therefore that capital punishment (which is very different from murder) is commanded by God for the crime of murder for this very reason. The murder of a fellow human being, made in God's image, is a heinous crime that warrants such a radical punishment. *"Whoever sheds the blood of man, by man shall his blood be shed; for in the image of God has God made man."* (Genesis 9:6)

To argue against the death penalty, even out of concern for judicial abuses on racial or political terms, or based on issues of human error—all of which are realistic concerns—is to disobey God's direct and clear command. As R. Kent Hughes describes it:

> Since man is created in the image of God and as such is of immense value, and since the blood (life) of man is God's alone, to take human life is to usurp God's sovereignty over life and death—and thus merits death itself. Precisely because life is so precious, the one who willfully takes another's life must suffer death at the hands of man.[30]

Such is the value and sacredness of human life created by God, made in His image and divinely given the significant role in the care of creation. Such is the basis of human exceptionality. Murder—and abortion and euthanasia—are monstrous crimes that reject our Creator God in abject defiance.

? QUESTIONS FOR CONTEMPLATION OR CONVERSATION

1. Why did God make male and female, and not just one or the other?

2. In what ways do we help each other to fulfill the purposes for which God created us?

3. In what ways is the current gender confusion a rejection of God Himself? How are we as Christians to respond to this confusion?

4. What is a human being in the mind's eye of the one Who created us?

5. What is a man and what is a woman to God Almighty?

6. How should we understand and preserve the sacredness of human life?

Part II

In this second section we will leave Genesis 1 behind and turn to several other Biblical texts, as we continue to consider what God has said about humankind we will begin with what God said through the prophet Isaiah.

CHAPTER 5

For My Glory

"Bring My sons from afar and My daughters from the ends of the earth—everyone who is called by My name, whom I created for My glory, whom I formed and made." (Isaiah 43:6-7)

Now we turn in a totally different direction, for another crucial question about our very existence. We have discussed that we are here because God created us. But, you might ask, **why** did He create us?

Christians believe that God is a self-existent, eternal, infinite Being, complete in and of Himself, needing nothing from humankind or from creation itself. As the Apostle Paul proclaimed in Acts 17:

"The God who made the world and everything in it is the Lord of heaven and earth and does not live in temples built by hands. And He is not served by human hands, as if He needed anything, because He Himself gives all men life and breath and everything else." (Acts 17:24-25)

And from Psalm 50:

"I have no need of a bull from your stall
or of goats from your pens,
for every animal of the forest is Mine,
and the cattle on a thousand hills …
If I were hungry I would not tell you,
for the world is Mine, and all that is in it."
(Psalm 50:9-12)

God does not *need* humankind in any way for His existence or completion. God is absolutely self-reliant and self-existent. "This attribute of God is sometimes called His self-existence or His *aseity* (a theological term taken from the Latin words *a se*, which mean 'from Himself')."[31]

Even the sacred name of God, given to Moses, "I AM" or "I AM WHO I AM," (Exodus 3:14), though truly untranslatable, is an expression of God's existence and character as coming completely from Himself and no one else. God always has been, and always will be, and He needs nothing from anyone or anything in His creation to be complete.

Some have claimed that God created humans because He longed for relationship and love. Does God *need* a relationship with us to feel loved and complete? As an author I read recently:

> "God was moved by love. He wanted to have an extended family, a people who could enjoy His goodness forever, a people He could love and who would love Him."[32]

That may be true, as far as it goes. But did God *need* people to love and who would love Him? Was the divine, Almighty, self-existing God of the universe lonely and in need of companionship and relationship? No, definitely not! Within the divine Trinity—Father, Son and Holy Spirit—there has existed through all eternity a relationship of perfect love, companionship and fellowship. He did not create us out of personal need.

Does God need our advice or input, in order to make right decisions about life in the present or the future? I cannot recall a single instance in all of Scripture where God spoke to Abraham, Moses, Isaiah or anyone else to ask their input or advice. He has certainly never spoken to me, saying, "Lenn, I'm confused. What do you think I should do now? Help me figure this out!" Rather, Scriptures attest:

> "*Can anyone teach knowledge to God, since He judges even the highest?*" (Job 21:22)

> "*For the foolishness of God is wiser than man's wisdom, and*

the weakness of God is stronger than man's strength." (1 Corinthians 1:25)

And my personal favorite:

"Oh, the depth of the riches of the wisdom and knowledge of God! How unsearchable His judgments, and His paths beyond tracing out! Who has known the mind of the Lord? Or who has been His counselor? Who has ever given to God, that God should repay him? For from Him and through Him and to Him are all things. To Him be the glory forever! Amen." (Romans 11:33-36)

God is *omniscient*, which means He knows all things and there is nothing that He does not know. Wayne Grudem writes:

"God's knowledge may be defined as follows: God fully knows Himself and all things actual and possible in one simple and eternal act."[33]

There is no darkness in God (1 John 1:5), there is no confusion or uncertainty or misperception or bewilderment or misunderstanding. God would never lose in *Jeopardy*, and He would be the perfect partner in any trivia game. He knows more than all the information in all the computers, encyclopedias (remember them?), scientific or medical manuals and history books ever written. There is nothing God does not know and He needs no advice or counsel from us. There is no philosophical, moral, ethical or scientific question too difficult for Him to fully understand.

A current technological obsession is to create Artificial Intelligence—AI. The theory is that we can program a super computer to have true intelligence, far above the capacity of any human mind, even the most cerebral among us. Some fear that we might eventually create a machine so far beyond us in intellectual capacity that it will come to rule and dominate us.

I'm not so sure about all of that. A computer is only as good as the information programmed into it, and it will therefore have the same biases as the one who programs it. Even beyond that, there will never be an AI computer to even begin to approach the wisdom, knowledge and intelligence of God.

Does God need our help to accomplish His purposes? Are there things too hard for Him that He needs our assistance to bring them about? We in the church sometimes talk about how we can (and maybe *must*) be God's hands and feet on this earth to help Him accomplish His purposes for the grand design of creation. But what does that really mean?

While it's true that God grants us the privilege and challenge of being used by Him for the purposes of His will, does He *need* us to do so, and is He incapable of doing it without us? No, God is omnipotent, He is Almighty. God is able to do anything and everything He desires, with no help from us.

When God told Abraham and Sara they would have a child in their old age (*well* beyond the age of bearing children), they were incredulous. Sarah even laughed at the very thought of it. God answered their disbelief: *"Is anything too hard for the Lord? I will return to you at the appointed time next year and Sarah* <u>will</u> *have a son."* (Genesis 18:14, emphasis mine) It was a rhetorical question, and the answer was no, nothing is too hard for the Lord.

Job complained long and hard, and challenged God over and over to answer for His actions (or lack thereof, in Job's mind). But when God finally came He never answered Job's questions or gave Job His reasons. He simply confronted Job with his lack of true wisdom, and Job humbly bowed before the Lord and cried out, *"I know that You can do all things; no plan of Yours can be thwarted." (Job 42:2)*

The angel Gabriel said to Mary, when she struggled to fathom how she could have a child when she was a virgin, *"The Holy Spirit will come upon you, and the power of the Most High will overshadow you. So the holy one to be born will be called the Son of God ... For nothing is impossible with God." (Luke 1:35-37)*

Clearly God does not need our help, thank you very much. He is more than able to do whatever He decides in His wisdom to do, and there will never be a shortage of power on His side of things. He will never run out of energy and need to be recharged, like our cell phones. He will never reach the end of His abilities. He will never find something too hard for Him to do and call out for our help.

So if God does not need our love and relationship, our advice and counsel, or our assistance and strength, why *did* He create us? Father, Son and Spirit have always been complete, full and fulfilled in and of Themselves. He/They did not *need* us in the least.

The verse above from Isaiah 43 tells the reason for our creation: "… *everyone who is called by My name, whom I created* **for My glory,** *whom I formed and made.*" (*Isaiah 43:7*, emphasis mine) That is an amazing statement by God, through His prophet, Isaiah. Let's put it into context.

God's chosen people, the Israelites, had been rescued by God from slavery in Egypt, led and provided for through the wilderness and taken into a land promised for them that was rich and fertile, all by God's almighty hand. He had established them there as a nation set apart to Himself, to serve as His priests and to show the world God's grace and power.

But they had failed, over and over again, and turned aside to serve and worship the false gods of the nations around them. So God sent a small army of prophets over the centuries, to call them back to faithfulness and to rescue them from foreign domination. But they continued to reject Him.

So God punished them … severely. But He had not completely rejected them. In Isaiah 42 and 43 (and elsewhere) God promised to send an ultimate Redeemer, who would one day come and save His chosen and called people from their sin, and bring them into a new, eternal Promised Land. He would, He said …

"Bring My sons from afar and My daughters from the ends of the earth—everyone who is called by My name, whom I created for My glory, whom I formed and made." (Isaiah 43:6-7)

In its context, that is referring first of all to the people of Israel. They were the ones God in His grace had chosen as His sons and daughters, and to whom this promise was directed. According to Matthew Henry's ageless commentary, the *Israelites* were the ones created for His glory, and they were formed according to the will of God, and these were the ones who shall be gathered in and returned to their land.[34] That is the context in which these passages were given and received.

By the way, God's chosen people were indeed brought back to their Promised Land in 1947 when the nation of Israel was reestablished, and it has since become a strong, vibrant and successful nation. Some nations of the Arab world around them have vowed to destroy them, but God's people remain. However, there is a broader application here as well, for the promise of an ultimate Redeemer was fulfilled in Jesus Christ. His salvation and rescue is for *all* who are predestined and called by God for salvation, and for all who will believe in Him as Savior. So the promises are for us as well ... and so is the statement regarding the reason for *our* very creation. *Israel* was created as a nation for the glory of God. *We* are also created for the glory of God. That is why we are here.

The Apostle Paul explained:

> *"In Him we were also chosen, having been predestined according to the plan of Him who works out everything in conformity with the purpose of His will, in order that we, who were the first to hope in Christ, might be for the praise of His glory." (Ephesians 1:11-12)*

As the people of Israel were chosen by God for the praise of His glory, so are we who are part of the elect body of Christ. Scott Christensen quoted John Piper:

> "God's chief end in creation and redemption is to display for the benefit of His elect the fullness of His glory, especially His mercy."[35]

Our creation and redemption was accomplished to display the fullness of the glory of God. When a person is saved from a life of wickedness, debauchery and immorality, to one of humble obedience and integrity, it brings glory to God. People can see what a change is wrought by the Spirit of the Living God when He brings about true repentance and newness of life. His forgiveness for sinners such as I shows His mercy and grace to the glory of His holy name.

We once knew a man who was a real scoundrel. He used and sold drugs, drank heavily, had an armament of guns in his home and often expressed his willingness to use them. He reveled in his reputation as a rebel and an all-round "tough" guy.

But after he suffered a very great emotional fall, God got hold of him and brought him to repentance and saving faith. Everyone who knew him or had heard about him was amazed at what God had done in him. His radically changed heart and life gave endless glory to the God who transformed him.

In the early 1900s there was what is now called the "great Welsh Revival." God's Spirit moved mightily in bringing countless people to repentance and changing their lives forever. Churches were full to overflowing with grateful worshipers. Workmen returned tools and materials they had stolen from work. Relationships were healed. Crime almost disappeared, and the police said they had nothing to do!

It was so dramatic that newspaper reporters from London went to report firsthand the marvelous happenings there. On their arrival in Wales one of them asked a policeman where the Welsh revival was. Drawing himself to his full height he laid his hand over his heart and proudly proclaimed: "Gentlemen, the Welsh revival is inside this uniform!" He had caught the holy fire.[36] People all around the world could see through these reports how God had moved, and He was given great glory and praise.

When a person gives generously (and hopefully in secret) to help another in dire need, it results in praise to God. The Apostle Paul encouraged the Corinthian church to give liberally for the needs of their fellow believers, and promised that their generosity would result in people giving thanks and glory to God for their provision. I'm certain that it did!

> *"You will be made rich in every way so that you can be generous on every occasion, and through us your generosity will result in thanksgiving to God." (2 Corinthians 9:11)*

When someone is miraculously healed of a deadly illness to the surprise of even the medical community caring for them, there is no one to praise but God Himself. During our pastoral ministry we once went to the hospital to visit a dying (so we thought) elderly man. He had slowly deteriorated to the point that it was clearly only a matter of time until he passed. The doctors and hospital staff had no more to offer.

As we walked down the hall to visit him (for the last time, we thought) we heard a voice laughing and talking. It sounded like him, but we could hardly believe it. But sure enough, when we got closer, we saw him sitting in a chair, laughing and talking with the staff, as vibrant and vital as ever. He had been on dialysis for weeks, but that was suddenly no longer needed for him. He soon went home in full health. Everyone was amazed and the doctors had no explanation, except to admit that it was a miracle. God was given glory for His intervention and blessing of this man.

When believers gather together on a Sunday morning to sing, pray and meditate on His Holy Word, glory is given to God. Indeed, that is what worship is!

How does your own life give glory to God? How can people see the hand of God in how you live and relate and care for people? Can people see that you have been changed by your faith in Him? Can they see the improvement He has made in you? Do you tell them that it was God who accomplished this in you?

Why are we here? Why did God create us? "Our purpose must be to fulfill the reason that God created us: to glorify Him."[37]

> "You are worthy, our Lord and God,
> to receive glory and honor and power,
> for You created all things,
> and by Your will they were created
> and have their being." (Revelation 4:11)

❓ QUESTIONS FOR CONTEMPLATION OR CONVERSATION

1. Does God *need* people to love and who would love Him? Is the divine, Almighty, self-existing God of the universe lonely and in need of companionship and relationship?

2. What does it mean that He chooses to relate to us and allow us to participate in His purposes?

3. Why are we here? Why did God create us?

4. How does your own life give glory to God? How can people see the hand of God in how you live and relate and care for people?

5. Can people see that you have been changed by your faith in Him? Can they see the improvement He has made in you?

6. Do you tell them that it was God who accomplished this in you?

CHAPTER 6

Fallen and Depraved

"The Lord saw how great man's wickedness on the earth had become, and that every inclination of the thoughts of his heart was only evil all the time. The Lord was grieved that He had made man on the earth, and His heart was filled with pain." *(Genesis 6:5-6)*

God is holy and perfect, without flaw, darkness or mistake. "God's perfection means that God completely possesses all excellent qualities and lacks no part of any qualities that would be desirable for Him."[38] He is flawless, with no wickedness or wrong in Him or in anything He says or does.

"Who among the gods is like You, O LORD?
Who is like You—majestic in holiness,
awesome in glory, working wonders?" (Exodus 15:11)

"As for God, His way is perfect;
the word of the Lord is flawless." (Psalm 18:30)

"... proclaiming, 'The Lord is upright;
He is my Rock, and there is no wickedness in Him'." (Psalm 92:15)

"He is the Rock, His works are perfect,
and all His ways are just.
A faithful God who does no wrong,
upright and just is He." (Deuteronomy 32:4)

So this perfect God created us, in His own image, male and female, to have dominion over His creation, and for His own glory. So that puts us in a very exalted place, right? After all, doesn't the Bible say just that?

> *"You made him a little lower than the angels;*
> *You crowned him with glory and honor*
> *and put everything under his feet." (Hebrews 2:7-8)*

However, as the Scripture passage from Genesis 6 above attests, there is more to the story than that. We also have to confront the undeniable fact that in God's eyes we humans are wicked and evil. He is perfect and flawless, we most definitely are not! We don't like to think of ourselves in those terms but it is true.

We were created and called to be perfect and holy as God is perfect and holy: *"Be perfect, therefore, as your heavenly Father is perfect." (Matthew 5:48)*. Maybe compared to other humans, we can believe ourselves to be pretty darn good. In an old movie we enjoyed, one character, a woman, asked a young boy how he is related to her boss. The boy says, "Pretty close." She asks, *"How* close?" He answers, "Pretty darn." So by comparing ourselves to other humans around us, we can believe that we are "pretty" good, even "pretty darn good" when it comes to our character and behavior.

Maybe we've never robbed a bank, or stolen a car, or murdered or raped anyone, so that makes us pretty good when compared to those who have done such things, right? The truth is that we are not. We are all infinitely far from good, when compared to the perfection and holiness of God Himself.

I think it was Dr. Billy Graham who used to illustrate this by saying that you and I might be on a beach on the west coast. And we might decide to throw a pebble to Hawaii. We both throw it as far as we possibly can; and you might throw it much further than I did. But we would both be infinitely far from hitting Honolulu. Just so is our goodness before God. You might be a much better person than I, but we are both still infinitely short of the perfect holiness of God.

Iain Duguid said it this way, in his commentary on Numbers:

"Some of our sins are deliberate, while others are the result of carelessness and thoughtlessness on our part. Some sin, such as failing to love the LORD our God with all our hearts and all our souls as we should, is virtually inevitable due to our weakness as fallen human beings. We are pervasively contaminated people on every level of our beings."[39]

The passage at the outset of this chapter comes from the Old Testament story of Noah and the ark. God had created all that exists, including humankind. In rather short order humanity had become incredibly evil and wicked. God saw how great the wickedness of humankind had become, and that every thought of their minds were inclined only to evil.

It was so bad that God regretted that He had even created us, and determined to *"… wipe mankind, whom I have created, from the face of the earth—men and animals, and creatures that move along the ground, and birds of the air—for I am grieved that I have made them." (Genesis 6:7)*

But then, purely by grace, God chose Noah to build an ark and determined to save Noah's family and a sampling of all birds and animals from the flood to come.

So someone might say, "OK, but that was hundreds, even thousands of years ago. We've come a long way since then, haven't we? Things aren't that bad anymore, are they?" Well, no, we haven't … and yes, they are.

Hundreds of years after Noah, God spoke through King David:

"God looks down from heaven on the sons of men
to see if there are any who understand,
any who seek God.
Everyone has turned away,
they have together become corrupt;
there is no one who does good, not even one." (Psalm 53:2-3)

And hundreds of years after the time of that psalm, Jesus' disciple John wrote:

"If we claim to be without sin, we deceive ourselves and the truth

is not in us. If we confess our sins, He is faithful and just and will forgive us our sins and purify us from all unrighteousness. If we claim we have not sinned, we make Him out to be a liar and His word has no place in our lives." (1 John 1:8-10)

A contemporary of John, the Apostle Paul, said it this way:

"What shall we conclude then? Are we any better? Not at all! We have already made the charge that Jews and Gentiles alike are all under sin. As it is written: 'There is no one righteous, not even one; there is no one who understands, no one who seeks God. All have turned away, they have together become worthless; there is no one who does good, not even one. Their throats are open graves; their tongues practice deceit. The poison of vipers is on their lips. Their mouths are full of cursing and bitterness. Their feet are swift to shed blood; ruin and misery mark their ways, and the way of peace they do not know. There is no fear of God before their eyes.'" (Romans 3:9-18, emphasis mine)

These and many other Bible verses we could quote declare the wickedness and sinfulness of all humankind. "Total depravity" is the theological term for it. Just look around as the culture disintegrates around us. Listen to the news, read the papers and the online reports, and see how chaotic, dangerous and wicked our world is becoming. As J. I. Packer defined total depravity:

"It signifies a corruption of our moral and spiritual nature that is not total in degree (for no one is as bad as he or she might be) but in extent. It declares that no part of us is untouched by sin, and therefore no action of ours is as good as it should be."[40]

We sometimes say that deep down inside everyone is essentially good. We speak of the "innocence of youth" and think of children before the age of accountability as pure and undefiled. However, the Bible's view of us is far removed from that idyllic picture of purity and innocence.

At the very beginning of creation, Adam and Eve sinned by disobeying God's direct command. With them, all humanity fell into a sinful, fallen state. Rather than being born in innocence, we are all born with a sinful nature, bent to do evil and prone to wickedness from birth.

As King David also said:

> *"For I know my transgressions,*
> *and my sin is always before me.*
> *Against You, You only, have I sinned*
> *and done what is evil in Your sight,*
> *so that You are proved right when You speak*
> *and justified when You judge.*
> *Surely I was sinful at birth,*
> *sinful from the time my mother conceived me."*
> *(Psalm 51:3-5)*

In that instance, David was repenting of his sins of adultery with Bathsheba, arranging the murder of her husband, and covering up his sins for political and personal expediency. But he also seems to have looked back over his life and realized that he was sinful at birth, even from the very time his mother conceived him.

The same is true of all of us. Whatever specific sins we have committed in thought, word or deed—and we all would have many to confess—we must understand that we were sinful at birth and even from the time we were conceived. As the late Dr. R. C. Sproul said it, "It's not that we are sinners because we sin, but rather, we sin because we are sinners."[41] According to God's timeless, Holy Word, that is who we are, by nature, from birth.

Paul affirmed this in Ephesians 2:

> *"As for you, you were dead in your transgressions and sins, in which*
> *you used to live when you followed the ways of this world and of*
> *the ruler of the kingdom of the air, the spirit who is now at work*
> *in those who are disobedient. All of us also lived among them at*
> *one time, gratifying the cravings of our sinful nature and following*

its desires and thoughts. Like the rest, we were by nature objects of wrath." (Ephesians 2:1-3)

Paul there spoke of our sinful nature and how we are all dead in our transgressions, objects of God's wrath. That does not mean that we are all living lives of open rebellion, wickedness and decadence. We can, with the help of societal influence, education and civil law restrain ourselves most of the time and live reasonably moral lives. We can fool some of the people some of the time, even ourselves.

However, that sinful nature remains, and in the deepest recesses of our hearts we remain corrupted and in a very real sense wicked. As Mark Twain was reported to have said, "Man was created a little lower than the angels, and he has been getting a little lower ever since."[42] This is true of all of us.

Three-year-old Alyson was preparing to go with her mother for a hamburger. She told her mother she wanted a cookie before leaving, but her mother said, "No, not now. But if you are good, you may have some when we come home." On the way, Alyson became fussy and started throwing a fit. When she calmed down and realized what had happened, she asked her mother, "Mama, have I blown my cookies?"[43]

The truth is that we have all blown our cookies. The Bible says that if we claim to be without sin, we deceive ourselves and the truth is not in us (1 John 1:8). If we claim we have not sinned, we make God out to be a liar (1 John 1:10). There is no one righteous, not even one; there is no one who understands, no one who seeks God. Everyone has turned away from God and we have all become corrupt (Romans 3:10-12).

That is the Bible's description of our depraved, sinful human nature. Everything we do, everything we think and say, even the good that we manage to accomplish, is tainted to some degree by sinful motives. There is nothing about us and nothing that we do that is entirely, 100% pure and holy. Our emotions, our desires, our goals and motives, our hearts and minds are all tainted by sin. As Dr. Sproul said it,

> "I've never done an action in my life where at the moment I
> did it I was loving God with all of my heart, with all of my
> soul, and with all of my mind. Any action I've ever done, any

word I've ever spoken has always been tainted by some degree of blemish and personal sinfulness."

According to John Calvin, everything that makes us human including our very soul is out of kilter because of sin. Every human heart is an abyss of confusion. The heart is so riddled with sin that even what appears to be good is really cloaked in hypocrisy and deceit.[44]

All this means that we have nothing to offer to God to commend ourselves to Him. We have nothing with which to purchase our forgiveness from Him or to secure our ticket to eternal heaven. *"You say, 'I am rich; I have acquired wealth and do not need a thing.' But you do not realize that you are wretched, pitiful, poor, blind and naked." (Revelation 3:17)*

Many people today believe that God will accept them and welcome them into heaven if they have lived good and moral lives relative to the people and culture around them. But no one can be moral enough or do enough good things to deserve God's approval. No one can earn or achieve eternal life in God's kingdom, because we are all totally depraved from the moment of conception.

It's true that most people are not as openly and blatantly wicked and evil as some we could mention—Hitler, Stalin, Mao, Pol Pot, Putin and others. This is a hard truth for us to comprehend, much less accept. We don't like to think of ourselves as depraved sinners, rightly under the judgment of our divine heavenly God.

But think of it, just the Ten Commandments for example. Have you consistently and without fail put your relationship with God and honoring His glory above everything else in your life? If not, you have broken the first commandment. Is there anything or anyone in your life that could be considered an idol that you worship or put before God? If so, you have broken the second commandment. Have you cursed God—used His name, or Jesus' name, as a swear word? Then you have broken the third commandment. Do you weekly observe a Sabbath day of rest, worship and prayer? If not, you have broken the fourth commandment.

We could go on down the list. Have you honored your parents and treated them with all due respect? Have you murdered anyone? Remember that Jesus said that if you are angry with someone in your mind it is the same as murder (Matthew 5:21-22). Have you committed adultery? Remember that Jesus said if you have looked at anyone lustfully, you have committed adultery (Matthew 5:27-28). Have you ever "borrowed" something from work? You have stolen. On and on it goes.

And that's just the obvious things from the Ten Commandments. How many other transgressions that we might consider lesser sins (but they aren't) are we guilty of? Unkind thoughts, evil wishes, covetous desires, ungrateful lack of response to a kindness, little white lies, negative innuendo against someone that offended us, lack of forgiveness, etc., etc., etc., etc.

We resist the thought that we are sinners, we argue for our goodness and righteousness, and fail to see the truth of the wickedness of our very nature. Dr. Martyn Lloyd-Jones explained why this is so:

> "You will never make yourself feel that you are a sinner, because there is a mechanism in you as a result of sin that will always be defending you against every accusation. We are all on very good terms with ourselves, and we can always put up a good case for ourselves."[45]

And Dane Ortlund adds a concise summary: "In other words, we don't feel the weight of our sin because of our sin."[46] Better still, as God Himself has said it:

> *"The heart is deceitful above all things and beyond cure.*
> *Who can understand it?*
> *I the* LORD *search the heart and examine the mind,*
> *to reward a man according to his conduct,*
> *according to what his deeds deserve."*
> *(Jeremiah 17:9-10)*

Not all of us are as intentionally evil as the following story illustrates. But, judged by God's standard of perfect holiness, we all fall short and stand condemned.

Years ago, a pregnant woman stood in the yard of her Baltimore,

Maryland, home and shook her fists at God. In a torrential rainstorm she shouted vulgarities at God and taunted Him to strike her dead if He did indeed exist. After lightning did not strike her, she turned to her family who had witnessed her tirade and declared victory because she had proven that God does not exist.

She would later tell her son, Bill, that she didn't care if he became a drug addict, bank robber, or brought home a boyfriend instead of a girl-friend, all she wanted was for him to never become a Christian.

But Bill Murray *did* become a Christian at age 33 and his mother disowned him. He had done the one thing she had hoped he never would. His life had been transformed from addictions to pornography and alcohol. He came to know the peace that had eluded him all his life. Bitterness began to loosen its stranglehold on his heart and he started giving to others for the first time in his life. None of that mattered to his mom. The only ambition Madalyn Murray O'Hare had for her son was that he *not* become a Chris-tian—even though it was the one thing that could heal him and lead to his peace and joy in life.[47]

Not many of us are that intentionally and openly antagonistic towards God. Not many of us are that stubbornly atheistic and wicked, even towards our own family. But all of us carry around that sinful nature that taints ev-erything we think, say and do. And none of us is as pure and innocent as we would like to think.

This is a hard reality for most of us to face. King David did not see this easily, either. He had, as we said earlier, committed adultery with (it could be said raped) a neighbor's wife, had the man killed and hidden the truth for some undefined time. He thought he had covered his tracks and it would all work out just fine.

But it did not. God knew it all, and sent His prophet, Nathan, to confront David with what he had done. David was forced to acknowledge his wickedness. He repented, confessed and begged God to forgive him (2 Samuel 11 and 12).

"When I kept silent,
my bones wasted away
through my groaning all day long.

For day and night
Your hand was heavy upon me;
my strength was sapped as in the heat of summer.
Then I acknowledged my sin to You
and did not cover up my iniquity.
I said, 'I will confess my transgressions to the LORD—
and You forgave the guilt of my sin'."
(Psalm 32:3-5)

Notice that all the while David tried to hide and deny his guilt before God, God's hand was hard upon him. There was a deep heaviness in his heart and soul. He groaned (at least inwardly) and he even wasted away physically.

But eventually God got through to David, and he repented. He acknowledged his sin and confessed his transgressions to God. God knew it all along, but David needed to face it and turn from his sin to God. And God forgave him. We would all do well to do the same as David, remembering ... "If we confess our sins, He is faithful and just and will forgive us our sins and purify us from all unrighteousness." (*1 John 1:9*)

Our sin is a bigger deal than most of us realize. It creates a bigger and deeper chasm between us and God than we can possibly imagine. We are sinners. He is the holy, pure, perfectly righteous God. Sin cannot exist in His presence.

> "The gulf between God and human beings is bigger than we might imagine. It's not just that He is infinite and we are finite, He is almighty and we are puny, He is omniscient and we know very little. All that is true, and it makes the possibility of true prayer extraordinary. But more than all that, we are sinners and He is the Holy One."[48]

However, that is not the end of the story. There is good news to come.

 **QUESTIONS FOR CONTEMPLATION OR CONVERSATION**

1.   How is your fallen, sinful nature exhibited in your thoughts, speech and attitudes?

2.   Do you think of children as being born in innocence or with an innate sinful nature? Why?

3.   Do you ever feel the true weight of your sin? When and why?

4.   When has God provided gracious forgiveness to you?

CHAPTER 7

Accountable

"Meanwhile, when a crowd of many thousands had gathered, so that they were trampling on one another, Jesus began to speak first to His disciples, saying: 'Be on your guard against the yeast of the Pharisees, which is hypocrisy. There is nothing concealed that will not be disclosed, or hidden that will not be made known. What you have said in the dark will be heard in the daylight, and what you have whispered in the ear in the inner rooms will be proclaimed from the roofs.

I tell you, My friends, do not be afraid of those who kill the body and after that can do no more. But I will show you whom you should fear: Fear Him who, after the killing of the body, has power to throw you into hell. Yes, I tell you, fear Him'." (Luke 12:1-5)

There is something else to consider in regards to our innate sinfulness, and the many sins we commit along the path of our lives: *we will be held accountable.* This is another uncomfortable truth—along with our total depravity—that we would prefer not to think about.

Many people prefer to think that when life ends, we simply die and everything—for us—ends. There is no afterlife, there is no heaven or hell, and there is no judgment. There is simply nothingness. "Life is hard, then we die," is how some express it, implying there is nothing for us after death.

In this way of thinking, we are not held accountable for anything we think, say or do in this temporal existence. We can behave as badly or as well as we wish, and there will be no punishment or reward. There is no such thing as eternal justice. The worst characters of human history, the most despicable, wicked, contemptible people who have done the most heinous evil will never face judgment for what they have done, beyond whatever legal penalties they may or may not face in this life.

There are those who prefer this awful injustice to the thought that they themselves might have to face their own judgment before their Creator. The Bible presents a truth that would be very unsettling for such folks.

In the story quoted above, from the Gospel of Luke, Jesus was speaking to His disciples, as well as to the great crowds that followed after Jesus hoping to see a miraculous sign or miracle. Jesus warned them to beware of several serious problems:

Hypocrisy	12:1-12
Covetousness	12:13-21
Worry	12:22-34
Carelessness	12:35-53
Spiritual dullness	12:54-59

It is in His discussion of the first problem—hypocrisy—that Jesus spoke some sobering words that can sound very harsh. He said that there is nothing concealed that will not be disclosed, or hidden that will not be made known. There is nothing we have said in the dark that will not be heard in the daylight. And there is nothing that we have whispered in someone's ear in the inner rooms that will not be proclaimed from the rooftop.

What was Jesus saying there? He was talking about *accountability*. He was saying that ultimately we will stand before God and have to answer for our words, our pride, our hypocrisy and our sins in particular and in general. We may think that what we have said was in secret, but it will one day be revealed. We may think that we have had prideful thoughts and attitudes that no one ever knew—but God did. And He will one day hold us accountable.

An old story tells about a certain agnostic farmer that once wrote to the editor of a local newspaper about an experiment he had conducted. He said, "In defiance of your God I plowed my fields this year on a Sunday. I harrowed and fertilized on a Sunday. I planted them on a Sunday. I cultivated them on Sundays and I reaped them on Sunday. This October I had the biggest crop I ever had. How do you explain that?" The editor replied, "God does not always make full reckoning in October."[49]

We may think we have gotten away with something(s) because nothing bad happened to us in the immediate aftermath. Maybe nothing happened for a very long time. No one seemed to notice. We may ourselves even have long forgotten all about it. But Jesus said here that even if it occurred in secret or in darkness, it will someday come to light before God.

The point is that God will one day hold us to account, and we will stand before His judgment. The specific sin Jesus spoke of in this instance was hypocrisy. Hypocrisy is to try to appear to be something we are not. It is "to give an impression of having certain purposes or motivations, while in reality having quite different ones."[50] It is to pretend, to put on a false façade, or to act with pretense.

We do this because we want to be accepted. We act or speak in ways we think others will appreciate, even if it is not what we truly believe or who we truly are. We do this because we are afraid of being rejected, or condemned, or ridiculed. In today's woke, cancel culture, we may be afraid to say what we truly believe because we don't want to face the ire and vehemence of those who will disagree.

"Jesus mentioned 'fear' five times in these verses, so He is teaching us that a basic cause of hypocrisy is *the fear of humankind*. When we are afraid of what others may say about us or do to us, then we try to impress them in order to gain their approval."[51] This fear is more prevalent and realistically valid today than ever before!

Jesus instructed His disciples to overcome this fear, and to avoid the sin of hypocrisy, by remembering that God is our ultimate judge and He will hold us accountable for this and every other sin we commit. The people around us may make us feel embarrassment, shame or ridicule; they may be able to cause us to be fired or marginalized; they may even have the power to put us to death for our beliefs. But God is the One who will determine our eternal destiny. He is the One who can condemn—or justify—our very eternal souls. It is to God alone that we are ultimately accountable. He said:

> *"Do not be afraid of those who kill the body but cannot kill the soul. Rather, be afraid of the One who can destroy both soul and body in hell." (Matthew 10:28)*

Jesus discussed all of this in Matthew chapter 25. Read through this chapter to get the full details. He began by telling the oft-quoted parable of the talents. A man went on a journey, called his servants to his side and entrusted his property to them. He gave different amounts of money to each servant, and instructed them to care for it while he was gone.

When he came home, he settled accounts with them. He called them to answer for how they had managed his assets in his absence. Some did very well by him, greatly increased his wealth and were richly rewarded. *"Well done, good and faithful servant! You have been faithful with a few things; I will put you in charge of many things. Come and share your master's happiness!"* (Matthew 25:21 and 23)

One servant, however, did quite poorly, making no effort whatsoever to increase his master's assets, choosing instead to simply hide them for safe-keeping. This servant was severely punished by being cast outside the camp, into the darkness where there was weeping and gnashing of teeth (Matthew 25:30). The point is, each was eventually held accountable and was rewarded or punished based on how faithfully they had served the master's interests.

Jesus then immediately applied this parable by comparing it to the final judgment of God, when Jesus will return in glory and gather all the nations before Him (Matthew 25:31-46). *"He will separate the people one from another as a shepherd separates the sheep from the goats."* As Johnny Cash sang it:

> There's a Man goin' round taking names
> And He decides who to free and who to blame
> Everybody won't be treated all the same …
> When the Man comes around.

He will praise and bless those who served Him faithfully—by caring for those in need around them—and will give them a great inheritance in the eternal Kingdom of God. What form that reward will take in God's eternal kingdom, I can't really say. But somehow, God will do right in eternal life by those who do their best in this earthly existence.

But those who did not serve Him will be cursed and sent into the eternal fire prepared for the devil and his angels. It is a fearsome portrait of the final judgment and the accountability we will all face at the throne of the King.

Bildad, one of the comforters who came to counsel Job in his distress, gave a horrid depiction of hell, the final destination of the wicked:

"The lamp of the wicked is snuffed out;
the flame of his fire stops burning.
The light in his tent becomes dark;
the lamp beside him goes out.
The vigor of his step is weakened;
his own schemes throw him down.
His feet thrust him into a net
and he wanders into its mesh.
A trap seizes him by the heel;
a snare holds him fast.
A noose is hidden for him on the ground;
a trap lies in his path.
Terrors startle him on every side
and dog his every step.
Calamity is hungry for him;
disaster is ready for him when he falls.
It eats away parts of his skin;
death's firstborn devours his limbs.
He is torn from the security of his tent
and marched off to the king of terrors.
Fire resides in his tent;
burning sulfur is scattered over his dwelling.
His roots dry up below
and his branches wither above.
The memory of him perishes from the earth;
he has no name in the land.
He is driven from light into darkness
and is banished from the world ...
Surely such is the dwelling of an evil man;
such is the place of one who knows not God."
(Job 18:5-21)

"Hell is the place of insatiable terror, or terror that goes on and on and is never satisfied."[52]

God Himself spoke of this with Noah. After the great flood had receded and Noah, his family and the animals disembarked the ark and scattered over the now dry earth, God blessed Noah and his sons and told them to *"Be fruitful and increase in number and fill the earth." (Genesis 9:1)*

But then He also spoke to Noah about not eating the lifeblood of the animals that were taken for food and said,

> *"But you must not eat meat that has its lifeblood still in it. And for your lifeblood I will surely demand an accounting. I will demand an accounting from every animal. And from each man, too, I will demand an accounting for the life of his fellow man."* *(Genesis 9:4-5)*

This is talking about protecting life—of animals—and especially of humankind, made in the image of God. And those who transgress will be held to account.

The NIV uses the word *"accounting,"* which is a fiscal term, referring to recording, summarizing, analyzing, verifying and reporting the status and results of a financial report. The investment firms that hold our retirement funds are always sending us long and detailed reports of our accounts. We don't have a huge amount, but it is divided among numerous different mutual funds. It seems that every day we get in the mail a report from one fund or another that we are invested in. We sometimes joke that we would get no mail at all if not for these financial accountings.

I try to read them and carefully analyze them to see how we are doing, but I must confess I don't really understand very much of what they are trying to communicate. I must trust our financial planner to do that and to know what's truly going on. In the same way God will carefully go over the accounting and report of our lives.

The Apostle Paul referred to this truth as well in 1 Corinthians 3. He used the image of an expert builder laying a foundation and erecting a building above it. But he said we must be careful what foundation we build upon and what structure we erect. The only true foundation is Christ Himself, and His Gospel of salvation by grace, through faith.

And we can build upon that, Paul said, a solid building using gold, silver and costly stones, or something made of wood, hay or straw. One will be solid and of great value, the other weak and ultimately worthless. But the point is, both will one day be shown for what they are, because the Day of the Lord will bring it to light. It will be tested and revealed, and we will either be saved or suffer loss. (1 Corinthians 3:10-15)

A central factor in the beliefs of many who claim to be atheistic revolves around this very factor. They refuse to accept the truth that God will bring their lives to light. They do not want to believe that they are accountable to anyone but themselves. They don't want to admit the fact of their need to face the judgment of their Creator. Some will openly admit this is so.

Iain Duguid writes: "As a character in Dostoyevsky's *The Brother's Karamazov* argued, if God does not exist, then everything is permissible. If there is no transcendent being to define for us what is right and what is wrong, then there can be no absolute right and wrong, only personal preferences."[53] That is exactly what many would wish.

But trying to deny it does not remove the reality of the coming judgment. It is real. Journalist Cal Thomas said it this way:

> "Not only is this the great debate in law, it is the great debate of history. Is man autonomous and free to do what he wishes, or is he created by God for a purpose and answerable to God for his life? All other questions are eternally irrelevant if the right answers are not given to these questions."[54]

The truth is that we were indeed created by God for a purpose, and we are indeed answerable to Him for our lives. Have we fulfilled that divine purpose for our lives, or have we not? The Biblical record is very clear on this. We will face Him some day and give an answer for our behavior and works.

Centuries ago, a man conned his way into the orchestra of the Chinese emperor. He could not play the flute but he dramatically mimicked the characteristics of a seasoned flautist. His charade afforded him a modest salary and a comfortable place to live. He enjoyed the trappings of his deception until the emperor decided he would like to hear a private solo from each musician in the orchestra.

In a state of panic, he took flute lessons, but couldn't learn fast enough.

In desperation he feigned illness but the court physician couldn't find anything wrong with him. On the eve before his presentation, he took poison and committed suicide.

The Chinese language was impacted by this true, historical event, and it has impacted the English language as well. Because of that situation we now have the phrase, "He refused to face the music." The truth is we will all someday face the music. God will individually hold us accountable.[55]

That can be a terrifying thought. To think that our guilty conscience will be brought to light. All the sinful thoughts, the unkind or even malicious words, the violent acts, the selfish motivations—all the depravity we discussed in the previous chapter—it will all come before our eyes and before God's face, and we will realize that we have no defense. We are guilty as charged, with no rationalization or excuse.

The colonial pastor Jonathan Edwards (1703–1758) presented a powerful sermon titled "Sinners in the Hands of an Angry God," in which he described the judgment seat of God and the horrors of the punishments of hell. That's us—sinners in the hands of an angry God. As he spoke, people fell on their faces and wailed in terror at the wrath of God to come.

That's the bad news: We are guilty, depraved sinners facing an ultimate judgment for our transgressions, which are many. *"The lamp of the* LORD *searches the spirit of a man; it searches out his inmost being." (Proverbs 20:27)* We may not like the idea, but there is an eventual accountability coming—*for all of us.* But there is good news also, and there is hope. God is not just an angry God, He is also a gracious and forgiving God. For the good news, read on.

? QUESTIONS FOR CONTEMPLATION OR CONVERSATION

1. Is man autonomous and free to do what he wishes, or is he created by God for a purpose and answerable to God for his life?

2. How do you feel about the reality of an ultimate accountability for your life? Confident? Fearful? Why?

3. Do you believe in a literal hell? Why, or why not? What did the discussion above concerning hell say to you?

4. Are you building your life on the one true foundation: Christ Himself, and His Gospel of salvation by grace, through faith? How are you doing that?

CHAPTER 8

Immortal

"At that time Michael, the great prince who protects Your people, will arise. There will be a time of distress such as has not happened from the beginning of nations until then. But at that time Your people—everyone whose name is found written in the book—will be delivered. Multitudes who sleep in the dust of the earth will awake: some to everlasting life, others to shame and everlasting contempt." (Daniel 12:1-2)

We often use the term "mortal" to describe human beings. In fact, the two words are sometimes used interchangeably. A human is a mortal being, in one sense, who will eventually die. If someone suffers a mortal wound, it means something that will sooner or later lead to death. Mortal combat means to fight until someone dies. The word generally means temporal, earthly and finite, with a definite beginning and an ultimate end point.

God is not mortal, He is *immortal*. In fact, He is infinite, with no beginning and no end. He always has been and He always will be. He always has and always will exist.

"Praise be to the Lord, the God of Israel, from <u>everlasting to everlasting</u>. Then all the people said 'Amen' and 'Praise the Lord.'" (1 Chronicles 16:36, emphasis mine)

From "everlasting" into the past, to "everlasting" into the future, God is.

We humans, on the other hand, are definitely not infinite. We are not *"everlasting to everlasting."* We had a certain beginning point. We did not always exist into the infinite past. We are mortal in the sense that we did not always exist, except perhaps in the mind of God.

However, we *will* live into an eternal future. We are *immortal* in the sense that our lives will have no end. Those who believe, as we discussed in the previous chapter, that when life ends, we simply die and there is no afterlife, there is no heaven or hell, and there is no judgment—their view flies in the face of the Biblical record.

The short passage quoted above comes from the divinations of the great Old Testament prophet Daniel. It is just a small vignette from the great visions the prophet was given concerning the times at the end of this temporary, present age. He spoke of events that were coming in the near future for God's people in that very day and age—the time of Antiochus, who was a major enemy of the Jewish religion itself, and a vicious persecutor of all who believed in the one true God.

But that very same prophetic word looked much further into the future, to the destruction of Antichrist by Christ's coming in glory in the end of these temporal days. Someday Christ will return to regenerate or renew His creation. There will be a new heaven and a new earth, and all things will be once again what they were first created to be.

And God's prophetic vision to Daniel includes some dramatic images of the separation of the peoples of earth based on their response to God's grace in Jesus Christ. There will be times of hardship and tribulation in those end times unlike anything the world has ever seen before. *"There will be a time of distress such as has not happened from the beginning of nations until then." (Daniel 12:1)*

However, those who have trusted in Christ, those whose names are found written in the book of God, will be delivered. They will be taken from this earth, many believe, in a "Pre-tribulation Rapture," to wait for the day of Christ's return to the earth in power and judgment. At that time, multitudes will awake, Daniel said, some to everlasting life, others to shame and everlasting contempt.

Note the word *everlasting*. It's the Hebrew word *'ô·lām,* which refers to that which is forever, eternal; pertaining to an unlimited duration of time, usually with a focus on the future, with no anticipated end.[56] All will be awakened at the end of days, said Daniel's vision, to an eternal, everlasting reality.

Some, who have trusted in Christ as their Savior, who have loved and served Him in this life to the best of their ability, and whose names are therefore written in God's book of life, will enjoy that eternity in a place of glory and joy in a regenerated earth. The Apostle John described it as best he could, based on his vision in Revelation:

> *"Then I saw a new heaven and a new earth, for the first heaven and the first earth had passed away, and there was no longer any sea. I saw the Holy City, the new Jerusalem, coming down out of heaven from God, prepared as a bride beautifully dressed for her husband. And I heard a loud voice from the throne saying, 'Now the dwelling of God is with men, and He will live with them. They will be His people, and God Himself will be with them and be their God. He will wipe every tear from their eyes. There will be no more death or mourning or crying or pain, for the old order of things has passed away.'" (Revelation 21:1-4)*

> *"I did not see a temple in the city, because the Lord God Almighty and the Lamb are its temple. The city does not need the sun or the moon to shine on it, for the glory of God gives it light, and the Lamb is its lamp. The nations will walk by its light, and the kings of the earth will bring their splendor into it. On no day will its gates ever be shut, for there will be no night there. The glory and honor of the nations will be brought into it. Nothing impure will ever enter it, nor will anyone who does what is shameful or deceitful, but only those whose names are written in the Lamb's book of life." (Revelation 21:22-27)*

In short, those who are redeemed by the grace of God, and by their faith in Jesus, will spend eternity in a place of indescribable beauty, peace and joy, in the presence of God, Christ and the Holy Spirit. As David joyously sang:

> *"Surely goodness and love will follow me all the days of my life, and <u>I will dwell in the house of the Lord forever.</u>" (Psalm 23:6, emphasis mine)*

"I will praise You, O Lord my God, with all my heart;
<u>*I will glorify Your name forever.*</u>
For great is Your love toward me;
You have delivered me from the depths of the grave."
(Psalm 86:12-13, emphasis mine)

From his deathbed, the great pastor and evangelist Dwight L. Moody was reported to have said:

"Earth recedes, heaven opens before me ... This is no dream. It is beautiful. It is like a trance. If this is death, it is so sweet. God is calling me and I must go. Don't call me back. No pain, no valley, it's bliss."[57]

On the other hand, those who have refused to bow before God in this life and who have rejected His Son as Savior, will spend eternity in a far different, darker and harsher place. The Bible speaks of a *"fire pit ... deep and wide,"* which the *"the breath of the LORD, like a stream of burning sulfur, sets ablaze."* (Isaiah 30:33) It speaks of a *"fiery furnace, where there will be weeping and gnashing of teeth."* (Matthew 13:40-42) It uses phrases such as *"unquenchable fire"* (Matthew 3:12) and a *"second death."* (Revelation 21:8) It's a place where unbelievers *"will be tormented day and night for ever and ever." (Revelation 20:10-11)*

I don't know about you, but that does *not* sound like a place I would want to spend an <u>eternity</u>! I have heard some say that they would not mind hell, in fact they relish the thought, because they will be with many of their friends there. I doubt they will think that once there!

C. S Lewis noticed a memorial stone with the following epitaph: "Here lies an atheist – all dressed up and nowhere to go." He commented: "I bet now he wishes it were so." If, by his refusal to trust and believe, he ended up in hell, I'm sure that he did wish for different circumstances in the afterlife!

But in all cases, the Bible speaks of the immortality of human beings. It clearly declares our eternal future life, either in heaven or in hell. The Statement of Faith of the Conservative Congregational Christian Conference says, in part, "We believe in the resurrection of both the saved and the lost; they that are saved unto the resurrection of life and they that are lost unto the resurrection of damnation." Both are raised to an eternal future. In His parable of the sheep and the goats, Jesus said, "*Then they* [the disobedient unbelievers] *will go away to <u>eternal</u> punishment, but the righteous to <u>eternal</u> life.*" *(Matthew 25:46, emphasis mine)*

Notice that in both cases above, Jesus used the word "eternal." This was the Greek version of the Hebrew word we mentioned above; this was the Greek word *aiōnios*, which refers to "an unlimited duration ... since all time."[58] Again it is highlighting the immortality of humankind.

So what does this say to us, this fact that there is an eternity for us somewhere or other, after this earthly life is over? I can think of several things.

First of all, it tells us that life on this earth is very preliminary, and exceedingly short, compared to the eternity to come. It may *seem* long, extensive, and sustained, but when seen in light of the infinity to come it is but an infinitesimal blip on the screen of history.

> *"All our days pass away under Your wrath;*
> *we finish our years with a moan.*
> *The length of our days is seventy years—*
> *or eighty, if we have the strength;*
> *yet their span is but trouble and sorrow,*
> *for they quickly pass, and we fly away."*
> *(Psalm 90:9-10)*

The average lifespan of a human being may have increased a bit, in some places on this earth. Perhaps it is even shortened in other circumstances. But sixty, or seventy, or eighty, or even ninety years is still a very small amount of time to live on this earth when contrasted to the eternity to come.

Dr. Martyn Lloyd-Jones expressed it this way:

"There is only one thing to do with time, and that is to take it and put it into the grand context of eternity. When you and I look forward, ten years seems a terribly long time. A hundred years? Impossible. A million? We cannot envisage it. But try to think of endless time, millions upon millions of years. That is eternity. Take time and put it into that context. What is it? It is only a moment. If you look at time merely from the standpoint of your calendars and your almanacs and life as you know it in this world, it is an impossible tyranny. But put it into God's eternity and it is nothing. 'What is your life?' says James. 'It is a vapor.'"[59]

Perhaps that should cause us to consider the temporary nature of this life and compel us to make the best use possible of whatever time we are allotted. We have just a small slice of time to make a difference for God's kingdom on this temporal earth, and we should not (cannot) waste time on things that are of secondary importance.

Dr. Dietrich Bonhoeffer was a pastor and theologian in Nazi Germany during the time of World War I and World War II. He left Germany for a short time for the safety of the United States, but almost immediately felt called by God to go back to his homeland to stand for Christ in that atheistic regime. He wrote:

"What was itself a wonderful expedition this morning to a female acquaintance in the country, i.e., the hills, became almost unbearable. We sat for an hour and chattered, not in a silly way, true, but about things which left me completely cold— whether it is possible to get a good musical education in New York, about the education of children, etc., etc., and I thought how usefully I could be spending these hours in Germany. I would gladly have taken the next ship home. This inactivity, or rather activity in unimportant things, is quite intolerable when one thinks of the brethren and how precious time is."[60]

Dr. Bonhoeffer was someone who felt intensely the priceless value of time, and the need to spend it on things that truly matter. He did indeed return home, led the Confessing Church's courageous stand against Hitler and his false church, and was ultimately hung for his role in a plot to assassinate the Fuhrer. He died relatively young, but he made his (limited) time on earth count for eternity.

All of this should cause us to evaluate our priorities and purposes for whatever time we have on this earth. A speaker I heard at a conference some years ago described the shift in focus and purpose in our western culture. In the early 1900s, she said our focus was on God and piety, or *deism as* she called it. In the 1950s it shifted to a focus on society, or, to use her term, *weism*. And in the 1990s it became an emphasis on self, or *meism*. Many who evaluate and comment on cultural trends would agree with this assessment.

What about you and me? Have we shifted from piety to "meism?" Has our focus turned inward and away from the priority of loving God and others, and serving the purposes of His Kingdom to meeting our own needs and desires? I'm not suggesting here a strict asceticism that rejects normal human needs and desires entirely.

I think we would do well to consider how we are investing the time we have been given on this earth, and on what we are spending those days and hours. Yes, we must meet certain needs and responsibilities on a human level, and would be remiss to neglect such matters. Obligations for self-support, to care for family, to respect our parents, etc. must be properly met.

But above and beyond that, how are we investing in eternity? How are we giving attention to the things of God and His kingdom?

"And why do you worry about clothes? See how the lilies of the field grow. They do not labor or spin. Yet I tell you that not even Solomon in all his splendor was dressed like one of these. If that is how God clothes the grass of the field, which is here today and to-morrow is thrown into the fire, will He not much more clothe you, O you of little faith? So do not worry, saying, 'What shall we eat?' or 'What shall we drink?' or 'What shall we wear?' For the pagans run after all these things, and your heavenly Father knows that you need them. But seek first His kingdom and His righteousness, and all these things will be given to you as well. Therefore do not worry about tomorrow, for tomorrow will worry about itself. Each day has enough trouble of its own." (Matthew 6:28-34)

? QUESTIONS FOR CONTEMPLATION OR CONVERSATION

1. What does it say to you that there is an eternity for us somewhere or other, after this earthly life is over?

2. What about you and me? Have we shifted from piety to "meism?"

3. How are we investing in eternity? How are you giving attention to the things of God and His kingdom?

4. How do you balance the needs of earthly life with the need to invest in eternity?

5. Try to think of endless time, millions upon millions of years. Can you even grasp what that will be like? How can you comprehend such an eternity?

CHAPTER 9

Redeemed

"Say to them, 'As surely as I live, declares the Sovereign LORD, I take no pleasure in the death of the wicked, but rather that they turn from their ways and live. Turn! Turn from your evil ways! Why will you die, O house of Israel?'" (Ezekiel 33:11)

Congratulations if you have made it this far into the book! Some of what we have been considering—such as depravity, eternity and accountability—may have seemed difficult, challenging, even harsh at times. An honest look at who we are as human beings, according to the Biblical record, is not always an easy, warm and fuzzy experience. But it is necessary to get the full, true picture.

Now we turn, however, to some more encouraging and uplifting realities. A good place to begin on that note is Ezekiel, chapter 33. Let's put the passage above into its proper context.

As Warren Wiersbe describes it: The Babylonian empire had conquered God's people, and in the year 606 B.C. had begun a series of deportations of the Jews; Daniel (he of the lion's den) was in the first such group. In the second deportation (circa 597 B.C.) was a young man named Ezekiel, then about twenty-five years old. He was taken to Tel-abib and lived in his own house with his beloved wife.

Five years after Ezekiel came to Tel-abib, he was called by God to be a prophet, and to speak to the people the words God gave him to speak. This was six years before the total destruction of Jerusalem in 586; so while Jeremiah, another prophet, was ministering to the people back home, Ezekiel was preaching to the Jews of the captivity in Babylon.[61]

Ezekiel's prophetic ministry spoke of God's judgment on Jerusalem, chapters 4 through 24; God's judgment on the surrounding nations, chapters 25 through 32; and of God's rescue of the Jews and His restoration of the kingdom, chapters 33 through 48. Chapters 1-24 were given *before* the siege of Jerusalem; chapters 25-32 *during* the siege; and chapters 33-48 *after* the siege. Though the prophet was in distant Babylon, he was able to see events in Jerusalem through the power of the Spirit of God. Ezekiel not only proclaimed God's message to the people, but he had to live the message before them.[62]

Their homeland had already been conquered and many of its people were led into exile. That was bad enough. But now, through His prophet Ezekiel, God was warning them that their holy, capitol city of Jerusalem was about to be totally decimated. The destruction that had begun years earlier would be completed and the city would be left in smoldering ruins. Imagine the despair of God's people upon hearing this news!

It was unthinkable. It was the depths of humility. Their once proud city was to be completely devastated. How could they bear it? All these years the people in exile had longed for a return to their homeland. They had hoped to someday go once more to Jerusalem for the sacred feasts and to worship in the holy city. Now there would be nothing to which they could return. The people who had avoided the earlier deportation and remained in Jerusalem all along were facing the loss of their homes and a horrible death at the hands of their enemies. It was news of the worst possible kind.

But in the midst of their wailing and cries of despair, God had another message for Ezekiel to pass on—in spite of all their past sins, which had led to God's judgments on them, God still cared for them. "A yearning, compassionate, divine tenderness was expressed by the prophet"[63] ...

> *"As surely as I live, declares the Sovereign LORD, I take no pleasure in the death of the wicked, but rather that they turn from their ways and live. Turn! Turn from your evil ways!"*

This was a message of pure grace. The people had sinned horribly, they had sinned persistently, and they had sinned in spite of repeated calls to repentance. They *deserved* the wrath of God. They *deserved* the desolation that was impending and about which Ezekiel had warned them. It would have been just and right for God to punish them so.

However ... that was not what God truly desired for them. He desired not their death at the hands of the cruel invaders. He desired not that they be carried off into exile. He took no pleasure in the announcement of wrath that He gave Ezekiel to proclaim.

What God desired was for the people to repent of their sins, to turn back to Him, and to live. Surely, in one sense this was literal. God wanted them to live and not to die. The coming judgment was conditional. Had they repented and turned back to God, it all could have been avoided. But they did not, and the disaster came as warned.

But even beyond that, God wanted them to live full, faithful, obedient, and blessed lives. He wanted them to enjoy the best joy, security and abundance this life has to offer. As Jesus said it:

> *"I have come that they may have life, and have it to the full."*
> *(John 10:10)*

That's the fullness of life God desired for His people, Israel.

It's the same thing God has said to His people down through the ages, even to the present, even to us. To those who have been predestined and chosen by God since before the advent of time, He says: "I have no desire in the death of the wicked, but that the wicked might turn from their ways and live."

We've talked in previous chapters about the wickedness and depravity of all of us human beings. None of us are righteous in God's sight. We have all turned away from God to follow our own devices and desires. We all deserve to hear a prophetic proclamation warning us of God's coming wrath.

But God is still offering His mercy and grace, to those who will repent:

> *"If My people, who are called by My name, will humble themselves and pray and seek My face and turn from their wicked ways, then will I hear from heaven and will forgive their sin and will heal their land." (2 Chronicles 7:14)*

Our hope for forgiveness and life as the sinful people we are lies only in the grace of God. *"Sola Gratia, Sola Fide, Sola Christos,"* the church reformers proclaimed; only by grace, only through faith, only in Christ. God has always been a gracious and merciful God. As God had revealed Himself to Moses:

> *"And He passed in front of Moses, proclaiming, 'The LORD, the LORD, the compassionate and gracious God, slow to anger, abounding in love and faithfulness, maintaining love to thousands, and forgiving wickedness, rebellion and sin.'" (Exodus 34:6-7)*

Some think of the God of the Old Testament as being full of wrath while the God of the New Testament is loving and kind. That's not exactly true. God has always been a God of justice and at the same time a God of love and mercy. As one commentator put it:

> The God of the Old Testament is as full of grace as the God of the New Testament, and that is because He is the same God. Grace runs throughout all of God's dealings with mankind.[64]

There is a balance we need to maintain here in our thinking about God. On the one hand, He is holy and pure, totally righteous and sinless. He makes no mistakes.

> *"As for God, His way is perfect; the word of the LORD is flawless."*
> *(2 Samuel 22:31)*

And as such, He cannot abide by evil and sin. He rightly judges and punishes sin and evil, and will do so eternally for those who insist on rejecting Him.

> *"Whoever has sinned against Me I will blot out of My book."*
> *(Exodus 32:33)*

This is only just and fair.

But we must balance this with the truth that we have been discussing in this chapter. God does not desire judgment and wrath. He does not desire the death of the wicked. He longs for us to repent and turn to Him.

And He provided the solution to our sin—Jesus. Jesus, God's Son, came to earth to pay the penalty our sin deserves. He carried our sins to the cross and died for them there. God placed on Jesus the wrath that we rightly deserve, and He proclaimed that all who trust in Jesus for their salvation will be forgiven. As the Apostle John spoke it:

> *"If we claim to be without sin, we deceive ourselves and the truth is not in us. If we confess our sins, He is faithful and just and will forgive us our sins and purify us from all unrighteousness."*
> *(1 John 1:9)*

It would be like a criminal standing before a judge. The verdict is announced: He is guilty. The crime was capital, so his sentence is death. But someone rises and says, "I will die in his place. I will take his penalty onto myself." And the criminal is set free ... if that is, he accepts the offer of his benefactor.

So it is with Christ. We were all justly judged guilty and sentenced to death. But Jesus stepped in, took the penalty for us, and bore the full weight of God's wrath in our place, because God desires not our death, but that we repent and turn from our wicked ways. When we do so, and turn to Him by faith in Christ, we will live.

Listen to Psalm 5:

> *"You are not a God who takes pleasure in evil;*
> *with You the wicked cannot dwell.*
> *The arrogant cannot stand in Your presence;*
> *You hate all who do wrong.*
> *You destroy those who tell lies;*
> *bloodthirsty and deceitful men the LORD abhors.*
> *But I, by Your great mercy, will come into Your house;*
> *in reverence will I bow down toward Your holy temple."*
> *(Psalm 5:4-7)*

R.C. Sproul explained it this way:

> "The reason we do not suffer God's condemnation is not because He sets the condemnation aside, rather, it is because the condemnation does not take place in us but in Christ. The good news of the Gospel is that God sent His Son to do what we could not do even with the help of the law. Such is the nature of His grace—grace for which our gratitude must never cease."[65]

And this is where our response to this grand truth must begin—with deep, humble, joyous gratitude. We have been pardoned! We have been forgiven our multitude of sins—not because of anything we have done but because of the desire and love of God to see His chosen people saved.

I read a story a long time ago in a Christian magazine. It told of one of the generals of Cyrus the Great, King of Persia. This particular general came home from a long campaign in a foreign battlefield and was shocked to find that in his absence his wife had been arrested and was languishing in prison, charged with treason against her country. The trial was to be held that very day.

The general hurried to the court of Cyrus, and the guards brought in his own beloved wife. She looked pale and anxious, and tried to answer the charges brought against her, to no avail. He husband, standing near, heard the stern voice of the Persian ruler pronounce the death sentence.

When the guards came to drag her away to behead her, the general ran forward and fell at the feet of the Emperor. "Oh, Sire," he cried. "Not she, but me. Let me give my life for hers. Put me to death, but spare my wife."

As Cyrus looked upon the general, he was so touched by the general's deep devotion and love for his wife that his heart was softened. He remembered, too, how faithful this general had been in his military service and gave the command that the wife should go free. She was fully pardoned.

As her husband led her out of the room, he said to her, "Did you notice the kind look in the eyes of the Emperor as he pronounced the word of pardon?" She replied, "I did not see the face of the Emperor at all. The only face I could see was that of the man who was willing to die for me." (unknown)

How much more should that be true of us? What other face will we see, when we get to our eternal home, than that of the God/Man Jesus, who died for us and purchased our pardon? How we will rejoice in His glorious presence! And how should we be doing so even today, as we look forward to that face-to-face meeting with our Savior?

Is our gratitude to Him being expressed in our worship habits? Do we rejoice to go to the house of our God to give Him praise, or is it a be-grudging duty we fulfill by dint of will? Do we lift our hearts and voices in heartfelt praise to the One who died in our place, or do we mumble along as we look at our watches as we count down the verses?

And do we express our gratitude by being people of grace ourselves? Do we forgive as we have been forgiven? Do we forgive our debtors as we have been forgiven by God? (Matthew 6:12)

Remember the story Jesus told in the Gospel of Mathew, chapter 18, about a king who wanted to settle accounts with his servants. A man who owed him a huge sum he would not be able to pay in a hundred lifetimes was brought to him. Since he was not able to pay, the master ordered that he and his wife and his children and all that he had be sold to repay the debt. But the servant fell on his knees before him and begged for mercy. The master took pity on him, canceled the debt and let him go.

But when that servant went out, he found one of his fellow servants who owed him a very minor debt and ordered payment. His fellow servant begged him for mercy, but he refused and had the man thrown into prison.

Other servants saw what had happened, they were greatly distressed and went and told their master everything that had happened. Then the master called the servant in. "You wicked servant," he said. "I canceled all that debt of yours because you begged me to. Shouldn't you have had mercy on your fellow servant just as I had on you?" In anger his master turned him over to the jailers to be tortured, until he should pay back all he owed. (Matthew 18:23-35)

Jesus' point was that we are like the servant who was forgiven an un-payable debt, because of our sin. But we have been forgiven it by grace, through the payment of Christ on our behalf. Should we not also show forgiveness and grace to those who have become our debtors? How willing are we to show to others the kind of grace God shows on a daily basis to us?

David Robinson, Hall of Fame basketball player, said, "Grace means kindness given to someone who doesn't really deserve it. That's a big part of my life, knowing that God has given me so much that I haven't necessarily earned." We could all say the same. We've all been given much that we haven't earned or achieved or deserved on our own. All that we have is by the gift of God. And the greatest gift of all is to have the debt of our sins forgiven, and to be welcomed back into the family of God.

That happens only when God, in His grace, sends His Spirit to work on our hearts to show our sins and our need for repentance, and then enables us to repent and turn back to God. When we do, God welcomes us home, wraps His love around us and rejoices in our return. *"I take no pleasure in the death of the wicked, but rather that they turn from their ways and live."*

"There is no darkness that Satan can create
that can shut the love of God out."
– Corrie ten Boom

? QUESTIONS FOR CONTEMPLATION OR CONVERSATION

1. How do you conceive the justice of God in His reaction to sinful people, like you and me?

2. What does it say to you that God, nevertheless, does not desire the death of the wicked?

3. You have been graciously forgiven a multitude of sins. How have you responded to that reality? Has it humbled you?

4. How do you rejoice in your salvation? What more could you do to express your gratitude?

5. List some things that God has graciously given you that you did not earn or deserve:

CHAPTER 10

Loved and Celebrated

"For God so loved the world that He gave His one and only Son, that whoever believes in Him shall not perish but have eternal life. For God did not send His Son into the world to condemn the world, but to save the world through Him." (John 3:16-17)

Karl Barth, noted theologian and author, wrote some monumental volumes covering all aspects of faith and Christology. It is said that he was once asked, during a question-and-answer session following a lecture he had given at a German university: "Dr. Barth, what is the most profound truth you have discovered in all your theological studies?" Without pausing for even a second, the noted theologian was said to have replied, "That Jesus loves me, this I know, for the Bible tells me so."

With all that we have said thus far, how does God feel about us humans? He knows our inner and total depravity. He sees our sinfulness. He created us in His own image, but that likeness has been horribly marred by our fall into sin. We were created for His glory but live mostly for our own. There is not one of us who is righteous and worthy to receive His approval, either now or in eternity. So where does that leave us in God's heart?

Surprisingly—perhaps shockingly—He *loves* us! How do I know that? How can you know that? We can know it because the Bible tells us so. From beginning to end, God continually speaks, tells, shows and expresses His love for humankind. Creation itself flowed from the love of God. When Adam and Eve sinned, God declared just punishment. But along with the specific judgment against Satan, He promised a Savior-Redeemer to come.

"And I will put enmity between you and the woman,
and between your offspring and hers;
He will crush your head, and you will strike his heel."
(Genesis 3:15)

He chose a people for Himself through whom He promised to bless all people and nations; He was faithful to that nation in spite of their constant rejection of Him; He ultimately brought the promised Redeemer through that family line to save all who would believe; all this and much more reveals Yahweh to be a God of love. *"God is love,"* the Apostle John definitively declared, and he was right. *(1 John 4:16)*

> *"The LORD your God is with you, He is mighty to save.*
> *He will take great delight in you,*
> *He will quiet you with His love,*
> *He will rejoice over you with singing."*
> *(Zephaniah 3:17)*

The above passage is from a prophetic oracle spoken about the city of Jerusalem, promising that God's exiled people will one day return and rebuild the decimated city, and God will once again take great delight in her and even rejoice over her with singing. Is it possible that His delight extends to *all* of His people, who have become members of His eternal family by adoption, through faith in His Son Jesus? Can you imagine God singing and dancing with joy over you?!

> *"The LORD appeared to us in the past, saying:*
> *'I have loved you with an everlasting love;*
> *I have drawn you with loving-kindness.'"*
> *(Jeremiah 31:3)*

This was spoken by God through His prophet, Jeremiah, to the people of Judah. Is it possible that God would also say something very similar to *all* of His people of all time? Can you believe that God has loved *you* with an everlasting love and drawn you to Himself with loving-kindness?

> *"Since you are precious and honored in My sight,*
> *and because I love you,*
> *I will give men in exchange for you,*
> *and people in exchange for your life." (Isaiah 43:4)*

This one is from a series of prophetic messages from God through Isaiah, assuring Israel that, in spite of their continuing rejection of God and His Word, He will one day deliver and restore them. "You are precious and honored in My sight," God said to them, "and because I love you, I will do this." Is it possible that God is also saying this to you and to me, who have been grafted onto the vine of God's chosen people because we have trusted in Christ?

I would suggest that all of the above are expressions of divine love that extend to all people of all history whom God has claimed as His own. Make it personal and think of those passages as speaking to you—He delights in *me*. He dances with joy over *me*. *I* am precious in His sight, and honored.

The Bible passage I chose to headline this chapter is perhaps one of the most well-known Bible verses of all time. Watch a football game on TV and inevitably, someone in the end zone will hold up a sign with John 3:16 on it in bold letters. They assume you will know what that means, or at least that you will know how to look it up and where to find it (assuming that you are curious enough to find out!).

> *"For God so loved the world that He gave His one and only Son, that whoever believes in Him shall not perish but have eternal life. For God did not send His Son into the world to condemn the world, but to save the world through Him." (John 3:16-17)*

God saw the desperate state of all humanity. He saw our sinfulness and our bondage to our fallen nature. He knew there was nothing we could do to free ourselves and turn things around. He so loved *"the world"*—τον κοσμον *(ton kosmon)*—the cosmos, the universe and everything and *everyone* in it. God loved humankind, the whole human race. As Paul said it:

> *"All this is from God, who reconciled us to Himself through Christ and gave us the ministry of reconciliation: that God was reconciling the world to Himself in Christ, not counting men's sins against them." (2 Corinthians 5:18-19)*

So He did for us what we could never do for ourselves. He sent His one and only beloved Son, Jesus into the world, to die on the cross and pay the penalty we deserve for our sins, and reconcile us to Himself. We can have eternal life with Him in His glorious, eternal kingdom by our faith in Christ.

Why did God do this remarkable thing for us? It was because of His love that He extended such amazing grace to us. Why did Jesus accept such a horrific death for you and for me? It was His love that drove Him to it.

"Very rarely will anyone die for a righteous man, though for a good man someone might possibly dare to die. But God demonstrates His own love for us in this: While we were still sinners, Christ died for us." (Romans 5:7-8)

"But because of His great love for us, God, who is rich in mercy, made us alive with Christ even when we were dead in transgressions—it is by grace you have been saved." (Ephesians 2:4-5)

"This is how God showed His love among us: He sent His one and only Son into the world that we might live through Him. This is love: not that we loved God, but that He loved us and sent His Son as an atoning sacrifice for our sins." (1 John 4:9-10)

See how Scripture reaffirms this truth over and over again? It was out of His love for us that God and Christ provided for our salvation. The ultimate and definitive expression and proof of God's love for us is the cross of Christ. Henry Blackaby said it this way:

"Never allow your heart to question the love of God. Settle it on the front end of your desiring to know Him and experience Him, that He loves you. He created you for that love relationship. He has been pursuing you in that love relationship. Every dealing He has with you is an expression of His love for you."[66]

God loves you with a deep and everlasting love. Never doubt that. Never forget that. Keep it in your heart at all times—even and especially when life gets hard and confusing. God loves you with a deep and everlasting love.

There is a legendary story about a nameless monk/priest in the Middle Ages who announced that he would be preaching the next Sunday evening on the love of God. The cathedral was filled with eager listeners. During those days they were much more accustomed to hearing about the wrath and judgment of God than about His love, so they were anxious to hear this particular sermon.

The priest silently waited until the shadows fell and the sunlight ceased to come through the cathedral's stained-glass windows. Then, when the last bit of light faded from the windows, he went to the golden candelabra beside the altar, took a lighted candle, and walked to a statue of Christ hanging on the cross. He held the candle beside the wounded hands, then the wounded feet, then the open side, and finally the brow, which had worn the crown of thorns.

The great congregation, deeply moved sat quiet and still. They had come to hear a sermon on the love of God. In the hush that fell, the priest blew out the candle. There was nothing more to say. The people did not find what they had expected, but far more. They saw for themselves the love that bears all wrong in such a manner that it takes it away. It was something they would never forget. (From a sermon by John A. Redpath, "Getting to Know God.")

The cross of Christ reveals the love, forgiveness and mercy of God in a way that should move us to profound gratitude and humility. Think about how the Creator of all that is, the perfectly holy and Sovereign LORD God of all that is, sees our sinfulness and loves us still. He knows our depravity and yet sent His Son to bear His wrath in our place.

Jesus spoke the words of John 3:16 in His discussion with a Pharisee named Nicodemus. So He illustrated it in a way that an expert in the Old Testament would understand. He reminded Nicodemus of a story in Numbers 21:4-9, which was certainly familiar to Nicodemus.

The nation of Israel had rebelled (again) against God. So to punish them, God sent fiery, poisonous serpents (ugh!) that bit the people. Many died. Moses interceded for the people and begged mercy from God. God told Moses to make a brass serpent and lift it up on a pole for all to see. Any person who had been bitten, needed only to look at the serpent on the pole, and they would be immediately healed. I'm sure it sounded very strange to the Hebrews, but those who believed and had faith enough to look up at that brass snake were healed and saved.

Jesus said that as the serpent was lifted up on that pole, so the Son of God would one day be lifted up on a cross. Why? To save us from sin and death. As someone said it:

> "In the camp of Israel, the solution to the 'serpent problem' was not in killing the serpents, making medicine, pretending they were not there, passing anti-serpent laws, or climbing the pole. The answer was in looking by faith at the uplifted serpent."[67]

"The wages of sin is death" (Romans 6:23) and all of us are guilty. But God sent His Son into the world not to condemn us but to save us. By acknowledging our sins and looking up to Him in faith, we can be saved and healed.

The cost of such love was enormous. God sacrificed His only and beloved Son, who had been His partner from before the beginning of time. The Son endured the full wrath of God as His Father turned His back on Him for the first (and only) time in all eternity. We cannot calculate or even conceive how great was the price that was exacted from both the Father and the Son. Such is God's love for you.

Perhaps Dr. Barth was right—the greatest theological truth we could possibly learn and understand is simply this: Jesus loves me, this I know, for the Bible tells me so!

? QUESTIONS FOR CONTEMPLATION OR CONVERSATION

1. What is the most profound truth you have discovered in all your studies into the Christian faith?

2. How has God showed His love to you?

3. Do you think of God as delighting in you? Can you imagine Him rejoicing over you with singing and dancing?

4. What does it say to you that God would sacrifice His own beloved Son to save you from the penalty for your own sins?

5. What causes you to doubt the deep love of the Father for you?

CHAPTER 11

Gifted

"His divine power has given us everything we need for life and godliness through our knowledge of Him who called us by His own glory and goodness. Through these He has given us His very great and precious promises, so that through them you may participate in the divine nature and escape the corruption in the world caused by evil desires." (2 Peter 1:3-4)

Not only are we redeemed (by faith in Christ) and loved and celebrated by God, but we are also greatly and abundantly gifted by Him. It would take many pages to list all the gifts God has showered upon us, in addition to life itself. Look at just some of them ...

Food and clothing	Matthew 6:25-34
Rain and changing seasons	Genesis 8:22
Peace (at least in this land)	Leviticus 26:6
Answered prayer	Psalm 21:2
Strength	Psalm 34:10
	Psalm 29:11
Wisdom and knowledge	Ecclesiastes 2:26
Rest	Matthew 11:28
Eternal life	Romans 6:23
Wealth	1 Timothy 6:17
Rescue from trials	2 Peter 2:7-9
Comfort	2 Corinthians 7:6

James said it succinctly, *"Every good and perfect gift is from above, coming down from the Father of the heavenly lights, who does not change like shifting shadows." (James 1:17).* All that we are and all that we have comes to us by the gift of God. Did you earn a lot of money in your lifetime? It was God who gave you the intelligence, ability and opportunities to do so. Did you enjoy relatively good health all your days? It was God who so blessed you.

Theologians speak of this as "common grace," as opposed to "saving grace." As Wayne Grudem defines it:

> "Common grace is the grace of God by which He gives people innumerable blessings that are not part of salvation. The word common here means something that is common to all people and is not restricted to believers or to the elect only."[68]

God's *saving grace* is that which awakens people to His presence, their own sin, the offer of forgiveness through Christ, and the impetus to accept that offer by faith. It is God working in us to enable us to admit our sin and need for a Savior, and causing us to turn to Christ for the answer. In that sense, saving grace is for those who will believe and not for those who reject God's Gospel.

God's *common grace* is another aspect of God's amazing grace, which is given to believers and unbelievers alike. Apart from the atoning work of Christ, these are gifts of God that are available to every human He has created. As Jesus said it:

> *"He causes His sun to rise on the evil and the good, and sends rain on the righteous and the unrighteous." (Matthew 5:45)*

The beauty of creation's oceans, lakes, streams, mountains, and forests, the abundant fruitfulness of the fields, orchards, seas and gardens, are all blessings that fall on the just and the unjust alike. King David agreed:

> *"The LORD is good to all;*
> *He has compassion on all He has made ...*
> *The eyes of all look to You,*
> *and You give them their food at the proper time.*
> *You open Your hand*

and satisfy the desires of every living thing."
(Psalm 145:9, 15-16)

There are countless blessings of God that are common to all creatures great and small, human and animal. We are gifted, indeed.

In addition to those natural blessings, when God created us as human beings, He gave to each and every one of us certain abilities, competencies, aptitudes and talents. Everyone has their own unique blend of skills in various areas that enable them to exist and thrive in this earthly life. You may be a wonderfully talented musician. You may have extraordinary intellectual powers of reason and depth of understanding. You may be a gifted athlete, or have incredible strength, or artistic aptitudes or an almost infinite array of other gifts.

All are blessings that come through the common grace of God to all His human beings. Unbelievers may not realize the source of their wonderful abilities, which is a shame, but that does not negate that God is the One who has gifted them in such a way.

But even beyond such common graces, we must recognize the special *saving grace* of God. Have you trusted in Christ to redeem you? Have you believed in Him as the one and only Savior and relied on Him to provide for your eternal redemption? That faith and that salvation are yours only by the grace of God. You did not earn it or achieve it, you did not make it happen by your own wisdom or spiritual discernment. It was a gift of saving grace from God the Father through Jesus the Son, by the inner workings of God the Spirit.

According to the Gospel of Matthew, chapter 16, when Jesus came to the region of Caesarea Philippi, He asked His disciples, *"Who do people say the Son of Man is?"* They reported that some were saying He was John the Baptist come back to life; others a resurrected Elijah; and still others, Jeremiah or one of the prophets. *"But what about you?"* Jesus asked. *"Who do you say I am?"* Simon Peter answered, *"You are the Christ, the Son of the living God."* And Jesus replied,

"Blessed are you, Simon son of Jonah, for this was not revealed to you by man, but by My Father in heaven." (Matthew 16:17)

This was a bold statement of faith, and Jesus was saying that Peter did not come by this conviction on his own, or by the wisdom of any human teacher. This was a revelation directly from God Himself. The only way Peter could have come to such a conclusion was if God's Holy Spirit had awakened his heart and prompted such faith in Peter.

The same is true for you and me. If you and I have come to a saving faith in Christ it is only because God has given us the gift of faith. Our belief in Christ comes to us not because we have achieved it or earned it by our wise deductive powers or through our many great works, but solely by the regenerating power of the Holy Spirit moving within our hearts. That is God's *saving grace.*

> *"For it is by grace you have been saved, through faith—and this not from yourselves, it is the gift of God—not by works, so that no one can boast." (Ephesians 2:8-9, emphasis mine)*

In addition, God offers other gifts to those who do believe, who have received the grace of salvation. During the great Exodus, after God had divinely freed His chosen people from slavery in Egypt, and as He was leading them through the wilderness on the way to their Promised Land, God gave His man Moses instructions for the building of the moveable tabernacle. This was to be the place where they would seek God, worship Him and offer their sacrifices to Him. He gave very explicit and detailed directions as to the size, shape, colors, contents and even the materials they were to use.

Then the LORD God Almighty said this to Moses:

> *"Then the LORD said to Moses, 'See, I have chosen Bezalel son of Uri, the son of Hur, of the tribe of Judah, and I have filled him with the Spirit of God, with skill, ability and knowledge in all kinds of crafts—to make artistic designs for work in gold, silver and bronze, to cut and set stones, to work in wood, and to engage in all kinds of craftsmanship. Moreover, I have appointed Oholiab son of Ahisamach, of the tribe of Dan, to help him. Also I have given skill to all the craftsmen to make everything I have commanded you: the Tent of Meeting, the ark of the Testimony with*

the atonement cover on it, and all the other furnishings of the tent'..." (Exodus 31:1-7)

God even told Moses whom He had chosen to do the creative and artistic work required in the fabrication of the tabernacle *and* that He had specifically gifted those men of His choosing to be able to do the work in a competent, qualified and skillful way. It was by the gifting of God that these men would be able to do what was asked of them. The end result was a beautiful and even spectacular "dwelling for God." Other Old Testament characters, from time to time, were given specific gifting from God for particular needs and tasks.

On the day of Pentecost (Acts, chapter 2) when the Holy Spirit of God fell on the church as a whole, it could be said that God has gifted His people in a much broader and more dramatic way even than in Exodus. Now *everyone,* not just a select few, who have trusted in Christ to be their Savior, and thus have His Spirit living within them, have some very special, *spiritual* gifts from God to enable them to serve and honor Him in an effective way. As Paul described it:

> *"There are different kinds of gifts, but the same Spirit. There are different kinds of service, but the same Lord. There are different kinds of working, but the same God works all of them in all men. Now to each one the manifestation of the Spirit is given for the common good. To one there is given through the Spirit the message of wisdom, to another the message of knowledge by means of the same Spirit, to another faith by the same Spirit, to another gifts of healing by that one Spirit, to another miraculous powers, to another prophecy, to another distinguishing between spirits, to another speaking in different kinds of tongues, and to still another the interpretation of tongues. All these are the work of one and the same Spirit, and He gives them to each one, just as He determines." (1 Corinthians 12:4-11)*

> *"Now you are the body of Christ, and each one of you is a part of it. And in the church God has appointed first of all apostles,*

second prophets, third teachers, then workers of miracles, also those having gifts of healing, those able to help others, those with gifts of administration, and those speaking in different kinds of tongues. Are all apostles? Are all prophets? Are all teachers? Do all work miracles? Do all have gifts of healing? Do all speak in tongues? Do all interpret? But eagerly desire the greater gifts." (1 Corinthians 12:27-31)

Notice that all these special spiritual gifts, given by the Holy Spirit to those who have trusted in Jesus, are to be used *"for the common good."* They are meant to enable us to participate in and contribute to the work of the Gospel, both within the church and in its mission to the world. All believers have something(s) they can do to help build the Kingdom of Christ and further the mission of His church. Some are gifted teachers, others healers, others prophets and pastors, others able to show great mercy and compassion, others are prayer warriors. All such blessings are from God and are to be used faithfully for the good of Christ and His church.

Paul used the illustration of a human body, with all its various parts and organs and functions. If one part is missing the whole body suffers for the lack of it. All are essential to the proper working of the whole. So it is in the church. The church needs *everyone* to step forward and use their individual giftedness for the common good, so that the whole can work effectively and efficiently.

So, all of this raises some profound questions for us. Do you daily acknowledge the abundant *common grace* gifts of God in your life? Do you praise God for the beauty of His creation, the abundance of His provision, and the kindness of His care for you? The fact that you exist at all is by His grace. The fact that you are still alive is by His grace. Can you move about? Can you see relatively well? Can you take nourishment and use it to energize your activity? All of this is by the common grace of God, and should call forth humble praise to His name.

And do you seek to discover opportunities for the use of your abilities to make a positive difference in your world? Do you try to make some contribution to society, not just to your own well-being? How are you using the talents God has given you to provide something of help to others, your family and your community?

And finally, have you discovered your special spiritual gifts, given through faith by God's Spirit, for the up-building of His body, the church? Are you endeavoring to assist your pastor and church to spread the Gospel and reach into the community with the compassion of Christ? Don't let those gifts from God go to waste! Use them, with His guidance and strength, to make a difference, as He so leads you.

The great apostle, Peter, exulted that God has given us *"everything we need for life and godliness through our knowledge of Him who called us by His own glory and goodness. Through these He has given us His very great and precious promises, so that through them you may participate in the divine nature and escape the corruption in the world caused by evil desires." (2 Peter 1:3-4)*

Everything we need: the Greek word means *"the totality … all, every, each."* Like when the great flood came and "took them all away" (Matthew 24:39); or like when "all the disciples deserted Him and fled" (Matthew 26:56). All things we need—everything—to live a truly spiritual life, *"even all that is necessary for the preserving, improving, and perfecting of grace and peace,"*[69] are ours through the gracious gifting of God. You, my friend, are one very gifted person! Therefore the only response that makes any sense is one of great humility and constant praise.

As the great English pastor and preacher Charles H. Spurgeon (1834-1892) dramatically said it:

> "Behold the superlative generosity of the Lord Jesus, for He has given us His all. Although a tithe of His possessions would have made a universe of angels rich beyond all thought, yet He was not content until He had given us all that He had. It would have been surprising grace if He had allowed us to eat the crumbs of His abundance beneath the table of His mercy; but He will do nothing by half measures."[70]

"From the fullness of His grace we have all received one blessing after another." (John 1:16)

QUESTIONS FOR CONTEMPLATION OR CONVERSATION

1.   What "common graces" of God do you most appreciate and enjoy? Why?

2.   How do you praise God for the beauty of His creation, the abundance of His provision, and the kindness of His care for you?

3.   Do you seek to discover opportunities for the use of your abilities to make a positive difference in your world? Do you try to make some contribution to society, not just to your own well-being? How?

4.   Have you discovered your special spiritual gifts, given through faith by God's Spirit, for the up-building of His body, the church? What are they, and how do you make use of them?

CHAPTER 12

In the Hands
of a Loving God

"Then the word of the Lord came to me: 'O house of Israel, can I not do with you as this potter does?' declares the Lord. 'Like clay in the hand of the potter, so are you in My hand, O house of Israel.'" (Jeremiah 18:5)

Perhaps one more word of encouragement is in order before we finish this brief discussion. The text above is part of a divine oracle given through the prophet Jeremiah. God told Jeremiah to go down to the potter's house, to watch him working at his wheel. The potter shaped the soft clay into the desired form for the pot, but it did not give the result he wanted. It was marred. It was misshapen. So he remolded the clay and started over, perhaps more than once, until he had it in the shape and size he had imagined for it.

As the prophet watched the potter work and rework his material, God said to Jeremiah, "Can I not do with you (the people of Israel) as this potter does? Cannot I mold and shape you as I please? And cannot I remold and reshape you if necessary?"

God then gave the illustration of His work in the nations of earth. He said that if a nation is evil and needs to be torn down and judged, He can and will do so. But if they repent, He can also choose to hold back His wrath and not do as He had warned. By the same token, if another nation is planned by God to be blessed and built up, God will surely do so; *unless* they do evil in the sight of God … *"then I will reconsider the good I had intended to do for it." (Jeremiah 18:10)*

What was the point? It was that the Lord God Almighty is ultimately and eternally sovereign. He can do with nations and peoples (individually and corporately) as He so chooses according to His own will and wisdom.

"See now that I Myself am He!
There is no god besides Me.
I put to death and I bring to life,
I have wounded and I will heal,
and no one can deliver out of My hand."
(Deuteronomy 32:39)

God brings death and life, God brings healing and injury. He is sovereign over the affairs of humans and nations, and no one can change His purposes or diminish His sovereign rule. He is the Potter—capital "P"—and we are the clay. We are in His hands.

Why were we born in the country in which we were born? Why was I born in the United States, and why was I not born in Russian or India or Peru? Why were you raised in the specific family of your origin? You could have been born into a very different home and lifestyle. Why were we born *when* we were born? We could have been raised in medieval, feudal European society, as peasants or serfs, or in early American colonial days as a backwoods settler. Why here, and why now?

It was because *God* decided our birth date, our family heritage, and our cultural milieu. As R. C. Sproul used to say, "What are the chances of something happening by chance? My answer to that question is 'Not a chance.'"[71] The theological term for this is "sovereignty." Sovereignty has to do with authority, rule and control. And in Biblical terms, it means that God, as Creator of all that is, has the ultimate authority to rule and control all He has made. Scripture affirms this over and over.

"Praise be to the name of God for ever and ever;
wisdom and power are His.
He changes times and seasons;
He sets up kings and deposes them.
He gives wisdom to the wise
and knowledge to the discerning." (Daniel 2:20-21)

"I am the Lord, *and there is no other;*
apart from Me there is no God.

I will strengthen you,
though you have not acknowledged Me,
so that from the rising of the sun to the place of its setting
men may know there is none besides Me.
I am the LORD, and there is no other.
I form the light and create darkness,
I bring prosperity and create disaster;
I, the LORD, do all these things." (Isaiah 45:5-7)

God gives wisdom and discernment to whomever He chooses. God changes the seasons and sets up and deposes kings according to His own purposes. The rising of the sun is in His hands. He forms the light and creates the darkness. He is sovereign over all things and all people. As the politician and theologian Abraham Kuyper said it:

"There is not a square inch in the whole domain of our human existence over which Christ, who is sovereign over all, does not cry: 'Mine.'"[72]

So what does this mean? It means that there is nothing that occurs in our lives, good or evil, that is beyond the hand of God. Nothing—absolutely nothing—is outside of His ability to rule and reign. As the 17th-century English Puritan Jeremiah Burroughs said it, "There is nothing that befalls you but that there is the hand of God in it."

Therefore, we can know that whatever is going on in our lives or around us, God's got this! I am sometimes tempted to despair over the declining state of our nation, as it turns ever more intentionally and defiantly away from its heritage and from God. I am often driven to distraction by our failing economy and our national debt, which threatens to be our downfall. I often look at the corrupt and incompetent political leaders who control our destiny (in human terms!) and I am moved to anger and disgust. But God's got this! None of it is beyond His power to use and to turn as He so chooses. Whatever happens, He has either caused it or allowed it because it works to fulfill His purposes.

I have seen this in my own life. My wife and I had pastored in a particular church for quite a few years. It was in an area of the country we loved, there were many people in the congregation who were very dear to us, and we often imagined spending the rest of our ministry in that wonderful setting. But it did not happen.

Through a series of circumstances, many very painful and disappointing, God took us away from that congregation. We eventually ended up in another place where we were blessed to be involved in an amazing community ministry to the poor that allowed us to have a great and positive impact for the Gospel in our city. God did that, by removing us from a place we would rather not have left, and taking us elsewhere, where in hindsight we could see He had done an amazing thing. It was in God's hands all along.

And when He moved us on from that congregation, He put us in still another church where we also were blessed to be allowed to minister to hundreds of children in the local elementary school and to plant seeds for the Gospel in their lives and in the lives of their families. Who knows what fruit will result from that effort? It was in God's hands all along.

It was kind of like Joseph, in Genesis 37-45, who was sold into slavery in a foreign land by his own brothers, wrongfully arrested and imprisoned, but eventually rose to high position in the government from which he was able to provide for the people in a time of severe famine. He was even able to provide for his own family, even the brothers who had so shamefully treated him, saying these profound and iconic words: *"You intended to harm me, but God intended it for good to accomplish what is now being done, the saving of many lives." (Genesis 50:20)*. It was in God's hands all along.

Think about the infamous betrayer, Judas. He turned Jesus over to the authorities—for money, out of political disappointment and impatience, maybe all this and more. Christ was ultimately arrested, tried, beaten and crucified. But He also paid the penalty for our sins and provided a way for us to be reconciled to God in the process. And He rose again on the third day, as God had planned since before the beginning of time. It was in God's hands all along.

So is my whole life, so is yours. Your very existence and your every life experience is under the sovereign rule of Almighty God. It's not always through dramatic, so-called "miraculous" means, either. God moves in the mundane, everyday events of our lives to providentially provide for, protect and keep us. We may not realize it until after the fact. We may not even recognize His hand at all. We may doubt His providence because from our perspective, things look more chaotic than carefully kept by divine grace. As R. Kent Hughes said it in his commentary on Genesis:

> "Here is reality. Real life is unfair. Real life deals out many in-iquities. Real life is filled with sin and sinners. Real wounds are everywhere. But the transcending eternal reality is that God is all-powerful and that His massive providence is at work in His children's behalf. Life brims with hope and optimism."[73]

We may never know how many accidents God protected us from, how many times He ordered our steps to avoid dangers, how many people He brought into or out of our life at just the right time to encourage and help us along the journey of faith. God is always, *always*, working in your life.

Again we turn to Dr. Hughes:

> "The story [Joseph in the Old Testament, Genesis 37] is about the hidden but sure way of God. God's hidden hand arranges everything without show or explanation or violating the nature of things. God is involved in all events and directs all things to their appointed end … What a God He is—because He is not just a God of the extraordinary but a God of the ordinary."[74]

And here's the kicker—He loves you and is working for your good.

> *"But God demonstrates His own love for us in this: While we were still sinners, Christ died for us." (Romans 5:8)*

> *"And we know that in all things God works for the good of those who love Him, who have been called according to His purposes." (Romans 8:28)*

God loves you more deeply than you can ever imagine, and He has good plans for you, your life and your eternity. You can trust yourself to Him without reservation and be totally secure in the assurance of His love and sovereign control. As an old song says:

> "If you can't trace His hand
> trust His heart."

Do I understand how God can rule over all peoples and nations, and work through them all for His good purposes? No, but I can trust Him even if I cannot comprehend such profound and mystifying truths. As I once read, "We play checkers, but God plays chess, as His billions of moves bring the world toward its culmination."[75]

Take heart, my friend. God's got this, whatever "this" is that is going on in your life. He loves you, and He is in control.

❓ QUESTIONS FOR CONTEMPLATION OR CONVERSATION

1.   What circumstances in the world around us cause you to be discouraged or even to despair? Why?

2.   When have you felt like your life was out of control and headed for a fall? What was happening, and how did that make you feel?

3.   When you think of God's sovereignty, does that cause you to be hopeful or intimidated? Why?

4.   How does it help you to know that you are in God's hands?

5.   Can you trust in God's love even when things in your life look bleak?

CHAPTER 13

Conclusion—Anticipated and Awaited

"Do not let your hearts be troubled. Trust in God; trust also in Me. In My Father's house are many rooms; if it were not so, I would have told you. I am going there to prepare a place for you. And if I go and prepare a place for you, I will come back and take you to be with Me that you also may be where I am." (John 14:1-3)

When we know that we are going to have guests, a lot of time is generally spent preparing. The house is cleaned, dusted, vacuumed, everything put in its proper place, and nothing left out of order. Effort is made to make sure we have things decorated nicely, with ornamentations appropriate for the current season. We want everything to be "ship shape" to make our visitors feel warm and welcomed in our home. We even will try to make sure the lawn is nicely trimmed! It's all an expression of how much we value our guests and look forward to their arrival. How glad we are when we hear their car pull up outside! Could this be an incomplete, earthly illustration of a heavenly reality?

The text above is a small part of Jesus' interactions with His disciples during His last evening with them before His death. They were all together in an upper room. Jesus washed their feet, as an example to them of humble, servant leadership. He predicted His betrayal, denial and arrest, shocking them all. He promised them the gift of the Holy Spirit to empower their ministry in His name, and He spoke many last words of instruction.

He also tried to comfort them for the ordeal to come. His crucifixion would rock their world to the core, and Jesus tried to assure them that in the end, all would be well. He encouraged them to trust in the sovereign Lord God Almighty, and to trust also in Him.

And He spoke of heaven. "According to Jesus, heaven is a real place. It is not a product of religious imagination or the result of a psyched-up mentality, looking for 'pie in the sky by and by.'"[76] Heaven is where God sits on His throne, surrounded by the elders, saints and angels. Heaven is where Jesus now sits at the Father's right hand and intercedes for us. It is real. It is not a figment of our imagination or merely wishful thinking.

Heaven is "My Father's house," according to Jesus' words to His disciples. And—this is remarkable!—it is home for all of God's children. It is where even today those believers who have gone before us enjoy life in the presence of God, and where we ourselves—if we are saved believers—will one day live for eternity.

Jesus said, *"In My Father's house are many rooms; if it were not so, I would have told you." (John 14:2)* The Greek word *mone* is translated here in the New International Version as rooms. In the King James Version it is said to be "mansions." It simply means "dwelling place" or "room," so I'm not thinking of it as a huge palatial country manor.[77] I'll be overjoyed with a simple room, thank you very much. Just to be there will be glorious!

And then, Jesus said, *"I am going there to prepare a place for you." (John 14:2)* What a remarkable thing to hear! Jesus is preparing a place for us, getting it all ready for our arrival. I'm not entirely sure what that means. I highly doubt that He is vacuuming and dusting, but somehow He is preparing a living space for all true believers, and I'm sure every one of them will be wonderful, beautiful and warmly welcoming.

That says to me, in addition, that Jesus is anticipating and awaiting our arrival, like we wait with joyful expectation for our guests to arrive. Jesus knows who His people are, He knows when we are coming to Him, and He is making things ready to welcome us home.

I think of the father of the prodigal son, in Luke chapter 15, who "ran away from home," and spent his inheritance in decadent, wasteful living. When he came to his senses, he returned home with a repentant speech in mind. But his father saw him coming at a distance, ran to meet him and joyously welcomed him home. A great feast ensued. Many have commented on the fact that the father saw him coming, while he was still a long way off (Luke 15:20), showing that the father was watching and anxiously awaiting the return of his wayward child.

Could it be that Jesus is likewise watching and anticipating our coming home to the places He has prepared for us? Could it be that He is anxiously looking forward to that day when He can welcome us into our eternal dwelling places? It appears to me as if there is joy in Jesus' heart when one of His comes home.

Luke said in his gospel that *"there is rejoicing in the presence of the angels of God over one sinner who repents." (Luke 15:10).* That means that whenever a person admits their sinfulness, bows before God in humble repentance, and trusts solely in Jesus to save them by His work on the cross and His resurrection, the angels in heaven throw a party. There must be a lot of partying going on in heaven!

And that's just when a person is saved from their sins and begins the long journey through this life to the next. Imagine the rejoicing that happens when that person arrives home to heaven!

> *"Precious in the sight of the Lord*
> *is the death of His saints." (Psalm 116:15)*

Heaven is surely a place of great joy and love. It will be an amazing, incredible and fantastic home.

For those who were blessed to live in peaceful homes and with loving, caring families—as the saying goes—"You ain't seen nothing yet." And for those not so blessed, who endured much colder, painful, abusive situations on earth—if you are a true believer you will hardly be able to believe the joy, peace, security and love that awaits you in the Father's house.

As Warren Wiersbe states it:

"Since heaven is the Father's house, it must be a place of love and joy. When the Apostle John tried to describe heaven, he almost ran out of symbols and comparisons! (Rev. 21-22) Finally, he listed the things that would <u>not</u> be there: death, sorrow, crying, pain, night, etc. What a wonderful home it will be—and we will enjoy it forever!"[78]

But Jesus is not just passively waiting, not just preparing places for us—He actually promised that He will someday come and get us! Of course, prior to that glorious day, many of us will pass through the shadow of physical death. It may in fact be very painful and difficult for some. But for those who are still alive when Jesus returns, it will be an amazing passage—without death—directly into Heaven. (See 1 Thessalonians 4:13-18). Come, Lord Jesus!

But this leaves one final, crucial question—one that we have hinted at and even referenced several times in the previous chapters. That question is: How can we be sure we will be among those who will go to be with Christ, either when we die or when He comes for His own? We talked about the horrible realities of hell. How can we make sure we don't end up there?

There is only one way—Jesus. The Gospel of salvation through Christ has often been described as *"The Romans Road:"*

Romans 3:23   *"There is no difference, for all have sinned and fall short of the glory of God."*

(See also Psalm 14:1-3; Ecclesiastes 7:20; Romans 3:10-14.)

Romans 6:23   *"For the wages of sin is death ..."*

(See also Exodus 32:23; Ezekiel 18:4, John 8:24.)

Romans 6:23   *"... but the gift of God is eternal life in Christ Jesus our Lord."*

(See also Ephesians 2:4-10; 1 Peter 3:18; Hebrews 4:16.)

Romans 10:9   *"That if you confess with your mouth, 'Jesus is Lord,' and believe in your heart that God raised Him from the dead, you will be saved."*

(See also John 6:44; John 14:6; Ephesians 1:3-12.)

The bottom line is:

- if we admit that we are sinful people (as all humans are—see chapter 6),
- who deserve the judgment and wrath of God,
- but we remember that God desires not the death of the wicked but that the wicked repent and live (see chapter 9),
- and believe and trust that by grace Jesus died to pay the penalty we deserve and rose again on the third day,

- we will be saved and enjoy eternity in God's glorious presence (see this chapter).

Jesus is the ONLY way. *"Salvation is found in no one else, for there is no other name under heaven given to men by which we must be saved." (Acts 4:12)* So if you have never done so, pray today to confess your sin, admit your need for God's grace, and trust in Jesus to be the One to save you.

And then, read your Bible daily to get to know Christ better, talk to God in prayer every day, find a good, Bible believing church where the pastor faithfully preaches through the Bible verse by verse, and begin to learn and grow in that faith.

Here's a good prayer to get you started:

Dear Lord Jesus, I know that I am a sinner and need Your forgiveness. I believe that You died for my sins and rose on the third day. I want to turn from my sin and I want to trust and follow You as my Lord and Savior. Help me to live from this day forward in and with and for You. Amen.

Endnotes

INTRODUCTION

1   E. Metaxas, *Is Atheism Dead?* (Washington, D.C.: Salem Books, 2021), p. 51.

2   M. Korda, *The Life and Legend of Robert E. Lee* (New York, NY: Harper Collins, 2014).

3   J. Swanson, *A Dictionary of Biblical Languages with Semantic Domains, Hebrew Old Testament* (Logos Research Systems, Inc, 1997).

3   M. Lloyd-Jones, *Let Not Your Heart Be Troubled* (Wheaton, IL: Crossway, 2009), p. 34.

CHAPTER 1

5   D. W. Hall and M. Padgett, editors, *Calvin and Culture: Exploring a Worldview* (Phillipsburg, NJ: P & R Publishing, 2010), p. 5.

6   P. Davies, *The Cosmic Blueprint;* quoted by Eric Metaxas in *Is Atheism Dead?* (Washington D.C.: Salem Books, 2021), p. 94.

7   Quoted by E. Metaxas in *Is Atheism Dead?* (Washington D.C.: Salem Books, 2021), p. 31.

8   R. K. Hughes, *Genesis: Beginning and Blessing* (Wheaton, IL: Crossway, 2004), p. 23.

9   Ibid., p. 33.

10   E. Metaxas in *Is Atheism Dead?* (Washington D.C.: Salem Books, 2021), p. 109-110.

11   J. E. Smith, *The Pentateuch*, 2nd edition (Joplin, MO: College Press Pub. Co., 1993), pp. 56-57.

12   R. Alcorn quoted in D. D'Souza, *What's So Great About Christianity?* (Carol Stream, IL: Tyndale Publishers, 2008), p. 15-16.

CHAPTER 2

13   R. Jamieson, A. R. Fausset, and D. Brown, *Commentary Critical and Explanatory on the Whole Bible, Volume 1* (Oak Harbor, WA: Logos Research Systems, Inc., 1997), p. 18.

14   R. L. Thomas, *New American Standard Hebrew-Aramaic and Greek Dictionaries: Updated Edition.* (Anaheim: Foundation Publications, Inc., 1998).

[15] J. Swanson, *A Dictionary of Biblical Languages with Semantic Domains, Hebrew Old Testament* (Logos Research Systems, Inc, 1997).

[16] R. Jamieson, A. R. Fausset, and D. Brown, *Commentary Critical and Explanatory on the Whole Bible, Volume 1* (Oak Harbor, WA: Logos Research Systems, Inc., 1997), p. 18.

[17] J. E. Smith, *The Pentateuch,* 2nd edition (Joplin, MO: College Press Pub. Co., 1993), pp. 56-57.

[18] R. K. Hughes, *Genesis: Beginning and Blessing* (Wheaton, IL: Crossway, 2004), p. 32.

[19] W. J. Smith, "The Fear of Suffering Is Driving Us Crazy," in *Epoch Times* (Wednesday, December 28, 2022), p. A14.

CHAPTER 3

[20] J. Swanson, *A Dictionary of Biblical Languages with Semantic Domains, Hebrew Old Testament* (Logos Research Systems, Inc, 1997).

[21] K. Strassner, *Opening Up Genesis* (Leominster: Day One Publications, 2009) p. 25.

[22] A. Lewis, "Battle at the Bottom of the Sea," in *World Magazine* (January 28, 2023), p. 65

CHAPTER 4

[23] C. Ash, *Married for God: Making Your Marriage the Best It Can Be* (Wheaton, IL: Crossway, 2016), p. 80.

[24] L. Crabb, *Men and Women: Enjoying the Difference* (Grand Rapids, MI: Zondervan Publishing House, 1991), p. 151.

[25] Ibid., pp. 137-138.

[26] W. Grudem, *Systematic Theology: An Introduction to Biblical Doctrine* (Grand Rapids, MI: Zondervan Publishing House, 1994), p. 16.

[27] M. L. Brown, *Has God Failed You?* (Minneapolis, MN: Chosen) p. 104.

[28] S. Dillon, "Dangerously Funny," in *World Magazine* (December 3, 2022), p. 48

[29] J. Chan Erikson, "Stumping Experts On Gender," in *World Magazine* (June 25, 2022), p. 35.

[30] R. K. Hughes, *Genesis: Beginning and Blessing* (Wheaton, IL: Crossway, 2004), p. 146.

CHAPTER 5

31 W. Grudem, *Systematic Theology: An Introduction to Biblical Doctrine* (Grand Rapids, MI: Zondervan Publishing House, 1994), p. 160.

32 M. L. Brown, *Has God Failed You?* (Minneapolis, MN: Chosen) p. 130.

33 W. Grudem, *Systematic Theology: An Introduction to Biblical Doctrine* (Grand Rapids, MI: Zondervan Publishing House, 1994), p. 190.

34 M. Henry, *Matthew Henry's Commentary on the Whole Bible: Complete and Unabridged in One Volume* (Peabody: Hendrickson, 1994), p. 1158.

35 S. Christensen, *What About Evil?* (Phillipsburg, NJ: P&R Publishing, 202), p. 334.

36 P. L. Tan, *Encyclopedia of 7700 Illustrations: Signs of the Times* (Garland, TX: Bible Communications, Inc., 1996), p. 1152.

37 W. Grudem, *Systematic Theology: An Introduction to Biblical Doctrine* (Grand Rapids, MI: Zondervan Publishing House, 1994), p. 441.

CHAPTER 6

38 W. Grudem, *Systematic Theology: An Introduction to Biblical Doctrine* (Grand Rapids, MI: Zondervan Publishing House, 1994), p. 218.

39 I. Duguid, *Numbers: God's Presence in the Wilderness* (Wheaton, IL: Crossway, 2006), p. 244.

40 J. I. Packer quoted in R. K. Hughes, *Genesis: Beginning and Blessing* (Wheaton, IL: Crossway, 2004), p. 586.

41 R. C. Sproul, *Now That's a Good Question!* (Wheaton, IL: Tyndale House Publishers, 1996), p. 148

42 J. Billings, *Mark Twain's Library of Humor* (Montreal: Dawson, 1888), p. 492.

43 *Mature Living*, February, 1994, p. 48.

44 H. Selderhuis, *John Calvin: A Pilgrim's Life* (Downers Grove, IL: Intervarsity Press, 2009), p. 193.

45 M. Lloyd-Jones, *Seeking the Face of God: Nine Reflections on the Psalms* (Wheaton, IL: Crossway, 2005), p. 34.

46 D. Ortlund, *Gentle and Lowly* (Wheaton, IL: Crossway, 2020), p. 68.

47 L. Strobel, "God Talk: What God Would Say to Robert Sherman," Seeds Tape Ministry, August 2, 1992.

[48] J. Woodhouse, *1 Kings: Powers Politics and the Hope of the World* (Wheaton, IL: Crossway, 2015), p. 251.

CHAPTER 7

[49] Phillips, *Exploring the Psalms* (Neptune, NJ: Loizeaux Brothers, 1988).

[50] J. P. Louw, and E. A. Nida, *Greek-English Lexicon of the New Testament: Based on Semantic Domains*, electronic edition of the 2nd edition, Volume 1 (New York, NY: United Bible Societies, 1996), p. 765.

[51] W. W. Wiersbe, *The Bible Exposition Commentary, Volume 1* (Wheaton, IL: Victor Books, 1996), p. 219.

[52] C. Ash, *Job: The Wisdom of the Cross* (Wheaton, IL: Crossway, 2014), p. 203.

[53] I. Duguid, *Numbers: God's Presence in the Wilderness* (Wheaton, IL: Crossway, 2006), p. 295.

[54] C. Thomas, *The Things That Matter Most* (New York, NY: Harper Collins, 1994), p. 111.

[55] M. Lucado, "A Heart Like This," UpWords Tape, #TS9702.

CHAPTER 8

[56] R. Jamieson, A. R. Fausset, and D. Brown, *Commentary Critical and Explanatory on the Whole Bible, Volume 1* (Oak Harbor, WA: Logos Research Systems, Inc., 1997), pp. 647-648.

[57] J. Pollock. *D. L. Moody* (Ross-Shire, Great Britain: Christian Focus Publications, 1997), p. 340.

[58] J. Swanson, *A Dictionary of Biblical Languages with Semantic Domains, Hebrew Old Testament* (Logos Research Systems, Inc, 1997).

[59] M. Lloyd-Jones, *Setting Our Affections on Glory* (Wheaton, IL: Crossway, 2013), p. 24.

[60] E. Metaxas, *Bonhoeffer: Pastor, Martyr, Spy* (Nashville, TN: Thomas Nelson), p. 303.

CHAPTER 9

[61] W. Wiersbe, *Wiersbe's Expository Outlines on the Old Testament* (Wheaton, IL: Victor Books, 1993), Ezekiel 1-36.

[62] Ibid.

[63] R. Jamieson, A. R. Fausset, and D. Brown, *Commentary Critical and Explanatory on the Whole Bible, Volume 1* (Oak Harbor, WA: Logos Research Systems, Inc., 1997), p. 606.

[64] P. Jeffery, *Opening up Ezekiel's Visions* (Leominster: Day One Publications, 2004), pp. 92-96.

[65] R. C. Sproul, *Tabletalk Magazine*, June, 2014, p. 33.

CHAPTER 10

[66] H. Blackaby, *Experiencing God* (Brentwood, TN: B & H Publishing Group, 1994), p. 12.

[67] W. Wiersbe, *The Bible Exposition Commentary, Vol. 1* (Wheaton, IL: Victor Books, 1996) p. 296.

CHAPTER 11

[68] W. Grudem, *Systematic Theology: An Introduction to Biblical Doctrine* (Grand Rapids, MI: Zondervan Publishing House, 1994), p. 657.

[69] M. Henry, *Matthew Henry's Commentary on the Whole Bible: Complete and Unabridged in One Volume* (Peabody: Hendrickson, 1994), p. 2434.

[70] Quoted in A. Begg, *Morning and Evening: A New Edition of the Classic Devotional Based on the Holy Bible, English Standard Version* (Wheaton, IL: Crossway, 2003), June 30, morning.

CHAPTER 12

[71] R. C. Sproul, *Now That's a Good Question!* (Wheaton, IL: Tyndale House, 1996), p. 187.

[72] J. Bratt, *Abraham Kuyper: Modern Calvinist, Christian Democrat* (Grand Rapids, MI: Wm Eerdman's Publishing, 2013), p. 195.

[73] R. K. Hughes, *Genesis: Beginning and Blessing* (Wheaton, IL: Crossway, 2004), p. 450.

[74] Ibid., p. 436.

[75] M. Olasky, "A Thanksgiving Meditation" in *World Magazine* (November 28, 2015), p. 64.

CHAPTER 13

[76] W. Wiersbe, *The Bible Exposition Commentary, Volume 1* (Wheaton, IL: Victor Books, 1996), pp. 349-350.

[77] Ibid., pp. 349-350.

[78] Ibid., pp. 349-350.

About the Author

After serving thirty-eight years as a pastor, as well as in denominational and community ministries, Lenn Zeller is now retired and living in Pennsylvania with his wife and ministry partner, Janeen. Retirement has given time for Mr. Zeller to do some writing, in addition to this book three others: *What God Has Said—About God: And How That Can Inspire Your Faith and Life; What God Has Said—About Jesus: How to Know the Truth About the Most Important Person in History* and *What God Has Said—About The Holy Spirit: And the Life and Power He Brings to Those Who Believe.* All are available on-line. This book you now hold, and the ones about Jesus and the Holy Spirit are available at Masthof.com.

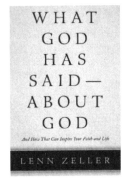

Who is God? What is God really like? How are we to comprehend and understand an infinite, eternal, and all-powerful being who is the resource and purpose of all that exists? It's not enough to believe that God exists, we must have an accurate and realistic understanding of God if we are to relate to Him in a meaningful and personal way. This book is written to help people have a correct, Biblical understanding of the person and character of God. (135pp. Amazon.com)

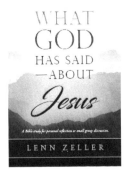

Who is Jesus, really? Can we even know the truth? Where can we turn for answers that we can believe? People have arrived at all kinds of different conclusions about who they think Jesus is: wise teacher, good man, spiritual guru, moral example, prophet, faith healer. Others, less charitable, have seen Him as a charlatan, liar, misguided fool, even mad. What matters is who Jesus is in truth. What is the truth about Jesus? Who is He in actuality? In this Bible study for personal reflection or small group discussion we will ask those kinds of questions of God Himself, turning to His eternal, infallible, universal Word of Truth—the Bible—for the answers. (134pp. Masthof Press, 2021.) *$12.00*

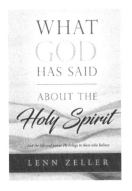

Christians talk about the Holy Trinity: God the Father, Son and Holy Spirit. Who is the Holy Spirit? What does He do? How can we know more of Him and relate better to Him? We will turn to God for the answers, focusing on passages in the Bible in which God Himself tells us something about God the Holy Spirit. In this age of information, with a plethora of sources claiming to know the truth, it is vitally important to verify the information you are receiving as accurate and correct. What better person to turn to than God Himself, in His perfect and timeless revelation? (144pp. Masthof Press, 2022.) *$12.00*